WORKING IN THE
VIRTUAL STACKS

WORKING IN THE
VIRTUAL STACKS

The New Library & Information Science

LAURA TOWNSEND KANE

AMERICAN LIBRARY ASSOCIATION | CHICAGO 2011

Laura Townsend Kane is the assistant director for information services at the University of South Carolina's School of Medicine (SOM) Library in Columbia, South Carolina. Kane is coauthor of *Answers to the Health Questions People Ask in Libraries: A Medical Library Association Guide* and author of "Access versus Ownership" in the *Encyclopedia of Library and Information Science*, several book chapters about librarianship career opportunities, and peer-reviewed journal articles on various issues in librarianship. She is an active member of the Medical Library Association (MLA) and its regional Southern Chapter, and is a Distinguished Member of MLA's Academy of Health Information Professionals (AHIP).

© 2011 by the American Library Association
All rights reserved except those which may be granted by Title 17, Sections 107 and 108, of the United States Code.

Printed in the United States of America
15 14 13 12 11   5 4 3 2 1

While extensive effort has gone into ensuring the reliability of the information in this book, the publisher makes no warranty, express or implied, with respect to the material contained herein.

ISBNs: 978-0-8389-1103-7 (paper); 978-0-8389-9326-2 (PDF); 978-0-8389-9327-9 (ePub); 978-0-8389-9328-6 (Mobipocket); 978-0-8389-9329-3 (Kindle). For more information on digital formats, visit the ALA Store at alastore.ala.org and select eEditions.

Library of Congress Cataloging-in-Publication Data
Kane, Laura Townsend.
    Working in the virtual stacks : the new library and information science / Laura Townsend Kane.
       p.   cm.
    Includes bibliographical references and index.
    ISBN 978-0-8389-1103-7 (alk. paper)
    1. Library science—Vocational guidance—United States. 2. Information science—Vocational guidance—United States. 3. Librarians—Employment—United States. 4. Librarians—Job descriptions—United States. 5. Librarians—Effect of technological innovations on. 6. Librarians—United States—Interviews. I. Title.
    Z682.35.V62K37 2011
    020.23'73—dc22

                                                                                        2011016135

Book design in Liberation Serif and Melbourne by Casey Bayer.

♾ This paper meets the requirements of ANSI/NISO Z39.48-1992 (Permanence of Paper).

CONTENTS

PREFACE

SEVEN YEARS. Not such a long span of time in the context of history. What can happen in seven years? Well, let's get some perspective. In seven years, my middle son went from infancy to being a very vocal second grader with a mind of his own. Wow, that happened fast. There's more: our family sold our old house, bought a new one, moved in, and had a third baby! In addition, I went from being a technical services librarian to being the assistant director for information services (in the same library). Okay, so a lot can happen in seven years.

What if we're talking about technology? How "long" is seven years in that context? Well, it's almost as if we're discussing dog years. These days, one year can seem like the equivalent of an *era* in terms of technological development. Let's do that perspective thing again. Think back: seven years ago, did you know what "BFF" meant? Did you have a Facebook or LinkedIn page? Did you have a talking GPS in your car? Did you imagine that your cell phone would ever do anything more than make and receive phone calls? Did you have an e-reader? Had you ever heard of Second Life or Twitter? Did you envision 3-D technology in your television? There could be hundreds more questions like these, and most likely your answer to all of them would be "no."

Seven years, then, technology-wise, is a long time. Now let's look at the profession of librarianship. Have the technological advances of the past seven years affected how we work, how we interact, how we live our professional lives? Absolutely! In amazing, unbelievable ways.

Working in the Virtual Stacks: The New Library and Information Science is a sequel to *Straight from the Stacks: A Firsthand Guide to Careers in Library and Information Science,* which was published in 2003. Though the first book featured interviews of some very tech-savvy folks, there was little mention of "social networking" or "embedded librarians" or "mobile devices." Today, there are librarians "out there" whose entire jobs revolve around such concepts! So much has changed. A librarian's job is more flexible than ever thanks to technology. Libraries themselves have gone through physical changes—some don't even have true "stacks" anymore and have gone completely virtual. Because of this, I saw a real need to produce a sequel to *Straight from the Stacks* that would illustrate how changes in technology have affected the work of librarians and the vision of libraries. Hence the title change with the addition of the word *Virtual.*

While on the one hand so much has changed, on the other, *not much has changed.* I am referring to the dismal fact that very few librarians seek out librarianship as a first career choice. This was the case in 2003, and it is still the case today. I have met many librarians throughout my career, and a common theme that crops up in conversation is the idea of the "accidental librarian"—those who stumble upon librarianship by accident (or fate!). As was the case in the first book, the librarians in this sequel either pursued librarianship as a second career or came across the possibility while looking for work in other areas. Many worked for years as student library assistants or library aides, until it occurred to them to make a career out of library work. Not one said as a child, "I want to grow up to be a librarian." This has always bothered me about my profession (even though I'm no exception, as I started out wanting to be a Spanish teacher). I do think, however, that this phenomenon is changing, but slowly. Librarians are taking a more active part in shaping the digital age; we are becoming more visible; we are reaching farther into academic and public communities; we are doing a good job adapting to change and making ourselves indispensable. So there is hope that our profession will soon rank right up there with "I want to be a firefighter when I grow up." Meanwhile, those of us in the field must do our part to help with recruitment by being more vocal about our fantastic profession. This book is my fulfillment of that charge.

The organization of this sequel is very different from the first book. Thirty-four interviews of librarians are arranged into broad categories reflecting librarianship *roles.* While *Straight from the Stacks* was organized by traditional library *type* (public libraries, academic libraries, special libraries, etc.), *Working in the Virtual Stacks* uses emerging roles as categories. The boundaries of library positions have somewhat dissolved—thanks in part to technology—so that it is no longer practical to discuss the profession in terms of traditional library type. To illustrate, a web services librarian can likely be found in a public library, a special library, an academic library, a corporate library, and in online businesses like Amazon.com.

This book, then, is divided into five chapters: Librarians as Subject Specialists, Librarians as Technology Gurus and Social Networkers, Librarians as Teachers and Community Liaisons, Librarians as Entrepreneurs, and Librarians as Administrators. The thirty-four interviews place spotlights on librarians from all over the country in all types of positions and reflect decades of collective professional experience. Most of these information professionals (as some like to be called) have had the unique experience of being witness to the birth and growth of the Internet, the explosion of social software, and the incredible expansion of the digital age. They have had firsthand experience of how technology has shaped libraries and affected the careers of librarians.

I will stress that this is by no means a comprehensive list of possible careers in librarianship. There are literally hundreds—thousands?—of possibilities out there for librarians, especially those proficient in technology and those who easily adapt to change. A comprehensive list would be impossible. It is my hope, though, that this book and its sampling of career possibilities will inspire two groups of people: those considering librarianship as a career and those considering a mid-career change. To those thinking about enrolling in library school, I hope you find sufficient excitement and intrigue in the text that follows. To those considering a change in librarianship positions, I hope you find your niche in the field; there is one for you, I promise!

I am once again in awe of the generosity of spirit that permeates those in the field of librarianship. The librarians featured in this book were eager to share their experiences—the good and the bad—with readers. I am a fan of each one of them, and I am proud to be associated with such an inspiring group of professionals.

To those of you reading this book, remember that a lot can happen in seven years—or five years or ten years. You never know where this profession might lead. Maybe *you* will be featured in the *next* sequel!

ACKNOWLEDGMENTS

I **WOULD** like to extend my deepest gratitude to the generous librarians who helped make this project a reality. I really believe that your willingness to share your experiences and your insights will help librarians make informed decisions about their career paths. You have been a joy to work with, and I am honored to have been associated with such an amazing group of professionals! Thanks also to my coworkers, my friends, and my family for your support throughout the completion of this project.

CHAPTER 1

LIBRARIANS AS SUBJECT SPECIALISTS

LIBRARIANS HAVE served as subject specialists throughout history. The concept is not a new one. Some of the most famous and influential librarians in history were proprietors of specialized collections of materials. Eratosthenes of Cyrene, the chief librarian of the great Library of Alexandria around 255 BC, could easily have been called a "subject specialist of classical antiquity."[1] As far back as the Renaissance, universities had learned librarians who were scholars in law, literature, or theology.[2] Saint Lawrence, patron saint of librarians and archivists, was a "subject specialist" of Christian treasures and documents, a job for which he was put to death by the Romans in AD 245.[3]

If "librarians as subject specialists" is associated with traditional, old-fashioned librarianship, why is it the first chapter in this book? "Why should I be interested?" you might ask. "Do we even need librarians as subject specialists anymore? I mean, I could just pick a subject and run a web search, right?"

Well, let's try something. Log into your web browser and run a simple query in the search engine of your choice. How many hits did you get? How much was junk? How much was legitimate, helpful information? A better question: just how long did you spend sifting through websites and following endless links before you felt that you had done sufficient "research"? Because it is so easy these days to access information, people are quick to jump to the conclusion that "subject specialists" and "information experts" are no longer needed. There is a term for this phenomenon, and it's called "disintermediation." (An aside: I just did a web search on "disintermediation" and spent six precious minutes browsing definitions and never found a good one related to librarianship.) This term—which basically means the elimination of the "middleman," that is, the librarian—recognizes that the Web appears to make an amazing range of information easily available to even the novice searcher. The friendly interface of the web browser, coupled with the power of search engines, creates the illusion of instant access to reliable data. However, while regular users of the Internet recognize the power of the Web, they are also aware of the limitations of current search engines, as well as the often inferior quality of the information retrieved. Librarians—or information professionals—are needed now more than ever to separate the "wheat from the chaff"—to systematically evaluate information in order to keep the good and eliminate the bad.

When dealing with subject-specific information, a librarian who is an "expert" in a particular field is invaluable. Would you trust information you find on the Web about health or law without first making sure the source is reliable and trustworthy? How would you know that, if you didn't have any experience with medicine or law? Could you sit down and run an effective search in a medical database without receiving any training? How could you be sure that you are using the correct terminology and that you've found all relevant database entries?

Librarians who are subject specialists have deep knowledge of a subject area, know the experts in the field, and are intimately familiar with their library's print and electronic collections. They also have an understanding of how information is organized and disseminated within a particular discipline, as well as how the information is retrieved and used by people who are active in the field.

There is no limit to career possibilities for librarians with subject-specific training. Whether you have a background or an interest in medicine, law, computer science, engineering, business, or astronomy, you have an advantage. Coupled with your advanced library degree, your subject-specific knowledge can open many doors of opportunity in librarianship.

ENVIRONMENTS

Until recently, the majority of subject specialists were considered "special librarians" who worked in "special libraries." Traditionally, these were medical, law, or corporate libraries. The Special Libraries Association (SLA), founded in 1909 as an organization catering to the professional needs of special librarians, no longer uses the term *special librarian* on its promotional materials. Instead, it has adopted the term *information professional,* which is defined as someone who strategically uses information in his or her job to advance the mission of an organization.[4] The term *information professional* is much broader in scope and illustrates that the boundaries of special librarianship have been erased.

Today, librarians with subject-specific expertise can be found in virtually any environment or organization, from academic institutions to government agencies to private corporations. Their place of work can be called libraries, information centers, competitive intelligence units, intranet departments, knowledge resource centers, or content management units. Though traditional "special libraries" still exist—law libraries, medical libraries, and corporate libraries—the subject specialists of today can be found anywhere.

RESPONSIBILITIES

The days of sitting for hours at the reference desk, waiting for patrons to approach with questions, are long gone. This stereotype, while appropriate for subject librarians ten or more years ago, is no longer even slightly accurate. Subject experts are faced with the challenge of "doing more with less" due to technological developments as well as changes in organizational structure. For example, in an academic library setting, subject specialists are increasingly responsible for liaison activities with specific patron groups. In many academic libraries, each professional librarian is responsible for resource development and liaison work within assigned academic departments. At Ohio University Libraries, for example, every faculty librarian is assigned "subject librarian responsibilities." The subject librarians are responsible for student and faculty orientations, emphasizing service based on knowledge of the subject area specific to their assigned academic departments. The librarians are expected to keep up with changing technologies and developing concepts within their assigned subject areas. They must be familiar with the curriculum, the research interests of faculty and graduate students, and the print and electronic collections relevant to the subject area—both within the library as well as outside the library. They are required to establish close working relationships with the faculty of their academic departments, and work with the departments on developing and maintaining collections of relevance to the discipline. The subject librarians also act as intermediaries between the academic departments and the library, addressing library-related questions and problems.[5]

The SLA "Career Center" website lists job opportunities for librarians with subject expertise. Some of the job titles listed currently are research coordinator, chemical reference librarian, American Craft Council librarian, information architecture librarian, head of science collection, knowledge services manager, and records management coordinator, among many others. Clearly the scope of responsibilities will vary depending upon the setting or institution and the patron/client base. There are certain responsibilities, though, that are common to many subject specialists, as described below.

Liaison with users. Today, there is increasing emphasis on "getting out there" rather than expecting users to show up with questions. This is especially true in this age of "Google mentality." Since people increasingly rely on their own information-gathering skills, librarians must make an extra effort to reach out to patrons. For the subject specialist, the emphasis is on connecting with users both formally and informally, teaching them how to use resources (especially electronic resources), serving as the expert searcher, and acting as a clearinghouse for subject-specific information.[6]

Reference/research. Technology has certainly made this responsibility exciting and diverse. As budgets for print collections have decreased, online databases and electronic journals have become the norm for research. Subject librarians must be comfortable with the terminology related to their field of specialization in order to effectively search databases and locate relevant information. They must also be familiar with how information is disseminated and used within the discipline. Since traditional "reference desks" are disappearing, there is an increase in "virtual reference," in which inquiries arrive in a variety of ways, including e-mail, IM (instant messaging), and social software applications such as Facebook or Twitter.

Collection development (print and electronic). Many subject specialists have the responsibility of building both print and electronic collections. Tight budgets require that the librarian select the resources that would be cost-effective as well as valuable to library patrons. Selection of e-resources is often more complex than traditional print ones and involves researching products, liaising with vendors, investigating hardware and software requirements, organizing trials and demonstrations, and coordinating purchases. Collection development also involves evaluating usage statistics.

Publicity and advocacy of the collections. Responsibility for publicizing subject-specific collections often falls to the subject specialist. This is closely related to liaison activities. Since the subject librarian often knows the strength of the library collections better than most users, it is up to them to encourage use; if people are not aware that a certain resource exists, it will probably not be used. Librarians act as advocates for new resources as well as the traditional ones, suggesting ways in which they might be used in learning, teaching, or research activities. Using the academic library setting again as an example, subject specialists might develop case studies for faculty that would encourage use of specific resources. Advocacy and publicity can often lead the subject librarian into the teaching process.

Teaching and user education. The importance of subject librarians as teachers is rapidly being recognized in many library environments. Who better to teach the use of resources, especially the electronic ones, than the librarians who are intimately familiar with the subject area and its related terminology? The best way to communicate the value of a resource or a collection is to teach users how to . . . well, use it!

Team involvement. Unless you are a solo librarian, you can expect to be involved in team projects. The days of the autonomous subject librarian are over. Subject specialists are often called upon to play a part in multidepartmental or multidisciplinary teams. Projects may involve research, development of new services, or any number of topics.

SKILLS

All of the above roles for subject specialists imply a number of traditional as well as newly adapted skills. Included below are the primary skills necessary for success as a subject specialist:

- subject expertise (learned on the job or through formal education)
- knowledge of the discipline or environment
- research skills within the discipline
- people skills
- communication skills
- teaching skills (public speaking)
- technical / IT skills
- financial management skills
- analytical and evaluative skills
- team-working skills
- project management skills
- flexibility (ability to adapt to change)
- ability to learn quickly
- vision

For a detailed guide on core professional and personal competencies, see the SLA's "Competencies for Information Professionals of the 21st Century" at www.sla.org/content/learn/members/competencies/index.cfm.

EDUCATION AND TRAINING

Generally, most positions require a master's degree in library and information science from an ALA-accredited institution. Specialized training in certain disciplines, such as advanced degrees, is sometimes required depending upon the position and the organization. Often an organization will support on-the-job training or continuing education. Law librarian positions sometimes require a juris doctorate (law degree), particularly for frontline reference positions. An M.D. is not generally required for medical librarians, although an undergraduate degree in a health-related field is sometimes necessary for clinical librarians in hospital settings.

PROFESSIONAL ASSOCIATIONS

Below is a list of associations recommended by the various librarians "spotlighted" in this chapter:

- American Library Association (ALA)—www.ala.org
  - *Association of College and Research Libraries (ACRL)*
    www.acrl.org
  - *Library Leadership and Management Association (LLAMA)*
    www.ala.org/llama/
  - *Association of Library Collections and Technical Services (ALCTS)*
    www.ala.org/alcts/
  - *Reference and User Services Association (RUSA)*
    www.ala.org/rusa/
  - *Public Library Association (PLA)*
    www.pla.org
  - *Business Reference and Services Section (BRASS)*
    www.ala.org/brass/
- Special Libraries Association (SLA)—www.sla.org
  - *Divisions by subject*
    www.sla.org/content/community/units/divs/index.cfm
- Medical Library Association (MLA)—www.mlanet.org
- American Association of Law Libraries (AALL)—www.aallnet.org
- Veterinary Medical Libraries Section of the MLA (VMLS)—www.vmls
  .mlanet.org
- Evidence-Based Veterinary Medical Association—www.ebvma.org
- Regional and local library associations

CATHERINE LAVALLÉE-WELCH

Associate Librarian and Director, University of South Florida Polytechnic Library, Lakeland, Florida

"It is very hard for a librarian to be a generalist in a large academic library. Having knowledge of a specific discipline helps to better serve library users and gain their trust."

CATHERINE LAVALLÉE-WELCH is the creator of the first blog focused on "sci-tech librarianship." In 2001, while working at an engineering, science, and technology library, Catherine created *EngLib: For the Scitech Librarian* (www.englib.info) to share information with librarians in similar subject-specific positions. The blog contained news items, updates on science and technology publications and databases, and information about job openings for science and technology librarians.

The name of the blog later changed to *EngLib: The Engaged Librarian* to reflect Catherine's current position as associate librarian at the University of South Florida (USF) Polytechnic Library. In this faculty position, Catherine is responsible for the administration and management of the library and its resources. The library supports USF Polytechnic programs, including engineering, business, education, information technology, and some disciplines from the arts and sciences such as psychology, criminology, and sociology.

"Our library has two faculty members (including myself), one full-time and two part-time staff members," says Catherine. "We could use more staff but Florida is in the grip of significant budgetary woes. I handle administrative duties as well as collection development, reference, research assistance, and bibliographic instruction. I'm also very active in university governance and participate in committees and councils, particularly those concerning technology. I typically attend three to five meetings per week, either related to governance or to various projects with other units. My current projects include the planning and design of a learning commons as the campus is expanding in a new location."

Catherine is invited to various classes at the beginning of each semester to teach library instruction to students. She also gives talks to new students during each orientation. "In addition, I hold at least four open-door seminars on database searching and citation management software per semester," she says. "I will soon be hosting the seminars online as well." She handles all marketing activities for the library and hosts library-related events twice per year, such as book drives and Banned Books Week programming. Her administrative duties include personnel management, budget preparation and management, and strategic planning, as well as day-to-day duties such as book acquisition, data entry, and supply orders.

The primary clientele of the USF Polytechnic Library are students and faculty. "The county where I'm located is still very rural and has pockets of deep poverty," Catherine says. "Many students have families and full-time jobs, and are often first-generation university attendees. Most have very little information literacy skills. It is sometimes difficult to reach all students for basic library instruction; some expect me to search all the information for them instead of me showing them how to do it themselves. We also serve community members, whose expectations are very often different—like the elderly gentleman who insisted on being able to check out books because he lived in town. He tried to convince us on three separate occasions. He still comes in but has learned to use the photocopier and scanner. One community user regrettably thinks our public access machines are an occasion to play online games for hours on end while talking on her cell phone. Diplomatic conversations are necessary in such situations."

Catherine says that her most rewarding accomplishment in her position thus far was the organization and opening of the first USF library on the Lakeland campus. When she first arrived, all library collections were housed in a nearby community college library (USF shares a campus with the college). "When I came in, my office was not in the library but among the university's faculty offices," she explains. "While a bit bizarre, it was great to really get to know the faculty. It greatly contributed to my rapid integration and the good relationships I have with faculty. I think it's important for academic librarians—especially those with faculty status—to be seen and acknowledged as colleagues by other faculty."

The plans for the new university library were already set when Catherine came on board, but she was responsible for ordering the furniture and supplies; space and equipment configuration; establishing services such as circulation, interlibrary loan, reserves, and so on; and acting as liaison with Information Technology Services with whom the space is shared. "Opening up the library was a rather unique experience," she says. "It is rare now that new academic libraries are created. Subject-specific libraries are more likely to be closed and integrated into a main library these days. For me, opening the first university library on campus was easily the most challenging and exciting thing I have done so far."

Solo librarianship is challenging for Catherine. "I have to adjust to new disciplines and I find it hard to fully answer the expectations of some of the users in those new disciplines," she says. "There is also never enough time to do everything that I would like to do. However, being in a small academic library does have its advantages. I have the opportunity to take on multiple tasks and services: create procedures, check out a book, erase a fine, process an interlibrary loan request, create an electronic reserve item, create a web page. These are things my colleagues at big campus libraries would never do. In a smaller library, you get a better chance to know your users more, even on a personal level."

Catherine enjoys "playing with technology" and manages to stay current. "When I was in library school, the LIS (library and information science) students were the first graduate students outside of the science departments to have access to the Internet. We would 'Gopher' and 'Veronica' our little hearts out in the computer lab. Our technology classes did not prepare us for this. I remember comparing the first versions of Cello and Netscape with a fellow student outside of class; those had just come out and our instructors had no idea. I jumped on the technology bandwagon, played a lot, learned from others, and built my career on it. I'm no expert but I think I did pretty well."

In addition to her *EngLib* blog and a "library services" blog, Catherine maintains Facebook, Twitter, Four Squares, and Flickr accounts for the library. "Social networks are important marketing tools for the library," she says. "They permit me to quickly distribute news about services, resources, schedules, and events. I've published library instruction screencasts for YouTube, and I have taught using synchronous electronic classroom environments." Recently, Catherine participated in a virtual job-shadowing project on Twitter organized by the Florida Library Association to help recruit new librarians. She posted "tweets" throughout the day to demonstrate a day in the life of an academic librarian.

Catherine received her M.L.I.S. degree from the Université de Montréal, the only French-language program accredited by the American Library Association. As an undergraduate, she majored in history with a concentration in records and archives management. "My goal was to work as an archivist," she explains. "I have an uncle who was an archivist and his work was so interesting. But the field is hard to crack. I worked for one year for one of my former professors in records management. Then I decided to go for my master's degree in archival management but decided to switch over to the library side for employment reasons."

While in library school and for a few years afterward, Catherine was involved in digital library projects with partners in French-speaking Europe. She worked as an information broker and as a consultant for various Internet projects for the nonprofit and cooperative sector. She also did a short-term contract at the library of the Pôle Universitaire Léonard de Vinci, a private business and technical school in Paris. In 2000 she got engaged and moved to the United States, where she took a job as an electronic resources and reference librarian at the Laura Kersey Library for Engineering,

Science and Technology at the University of Louisville. "Before coming to Louisville, my only contact with STM (science, technology, and medicine) clientele was when I was an information broker and had a corporate client in the food science industry. I feel that I was hired at the Kersey Library for my computer skills rather than my subject skills. I did a lot of work with databases and electronic resources and I also managed the computer lab and the website." She took her current position at USF Polytechnic five years later.

Catherine is very active in the Special Libraries Association and attends its annual conferences, webinars, and continuing education classes. She is a past chair of SLA's Information Technology Division and is a member of the Science and Technology Division, the Academic Division, the Engineering Division, the Baseball Caucus, and the Florida and Caribbean Chapter. She is also a member of the American Library Association, the Association of College and Research Libraries, the Library Leadership and Management Association, and the Florida Library Association.

To those interested in subject-specific librarianship, Catherine says, "I would argue that a librarian doesn't necessarily have to have a degree in the discipline served. I don't have a science or engineering degree yet worked in an engineering/science library. But it absolutely requires time and motivation on the part of the librarian to learn the discipline, its vocabulary, its evolution, its classic sources of information, and its novel sources of information—to better serve the library users and to gain their trust. The librarian isn't expected to know the details of the discipline, but he or she should be able to understand what the information needs are and where the information fits. If that means stalking the reference shelves for hours and spending time reading journal tables of contents (like I did), so be it."

Catherine says that important skills for any librarian are curiosity, creativity, and tenacity. People skills and stress management skills are essential. "A certain feel for office politics is necessary, especially if you have administrative functions, as well as a certain finesse to massage faculty prickly egos," she says. "For administrators, you must be able to prepare and manage a budget, personnel, and planning.

"While studying for your master's degree (or before), work in a library, particularly an academic one," Catherine continues. "This will be a big advantage in your vitae over other candidates. Get involved in a professional association; that will show promise for future service activities, which is important for most academic librarians. Try to transform a school paper into an article for publication in an ALA or SLA publication. Geographic mobility helps for finding employment, especially for that first job. Don't just consider the salary but also if the context—the library and the university—is a good fit for you. Consider cost of living.

"The M.L.I.S. degree can offer many different job titles and job duties," Catherine concludes. "Don't just stop at 'librarian.'"

Catherine recommends the following websites:

- http://stlq.info (*STLQ: The SciTech Library Question* blog)
- http://scienceblogs.com/confessions/ (*Confessions of a Science Librarian* blog)
- www.library.drexel.edu/blogs/englibrary/ (*Englibrary:* Drexel University's engineering resources blog)
- www.englib.info (Catherine's *EngLib* blog)
- http://catherin.blog.usf.edu (USF Polytechnic Library blog)
- http://librarydayinthelife.pbworks.com (a wiki work space for sharing the joys and challenges of working in a library)

LYNN BALTIMORE

Clinical/Reference Librarian, George F. Smith Library of the Health Sciences,
University of Medicine and Dentistry of New Jersey, Newark, New Jersey

"What is most unique about my job is that I actually see patients at the hospital bedside and have an indirect role in their patient care."

LYNN BALTIMORE has learned not to be squeamish. She has no problem eating a sandwich while watching a lunchtime PowerPoint presentation filled with vivid slides of tumors or open wounds. She once watched—without being sick—as a surgeon sutured the head of a man who had been hit by a car and thrown through a store window. No, she is not a nurse or a physician. She is a clinical librarian.

Lynn's full title is clinical/reference librarian at the University of Medicine and Dentistry of New Jersey (UMDNJ). Her job duties vary widely. She prepares lesson plans and teaches database searching—MEDLINE, PsychINFO, and CINAHL (Cumulative Index to Nursing and Health Literature), for example—to various library patrons. She teaches bibliographic instruction, focusing on accessing electronic journals and books and searching the online catalog, and has been involved in book collection development. "Each day I have a couple of hours of reference desk duty," she says. "Our reference desk is staffed by me and five other colleagues from Monday to Friday, 8 a.m. to 6 p.m. I also help to cover the public library and academic library queues in 'Q&A New Jersey,' a virtual reference service for New Jersey residents. The questions in the public library queue run the gamut from high school students seeking help with homework assignments to adults asking how to apply for unemployment. The academic queue consists of questions asked by students at community colleges and universities in the state."

As the only clinical librarian at UMDNJ, Lynn is pulled in many directions as she tries to meet the information needs of the various departments of the University Hospital. Possibly the most complex—and rewarding—of her duties was her involvement in patient care rounds for a number of years. "Once a week I attended patient care rounds in the sixteen-bed Surgical Intensive Care Unit," she recounts. "Often I went to the surgery morning report where the history and physical examination findings for each surgical admission were briefly reviewed. I usually spent three to four hours in the unit. Two beds in the unit were for transplantation patients, and the others were for a multitude of other surgical conditions such as falls, motorcycle or car accidents, or gunshot wounds. The patient care rounds were led by a surgery/trauma attending (there were six on a rotating schedule). The rest of the team included medical students, surgery or anesthesiology residents, oral and maxillofacial residents, surgical intensive care fellows, visiting students, and a doctor of pharmacology . . . and me! Specific details of each patient were discussed: admission date, reason for admission, ventilator settings, input and output volumes of urine and stool, status of the surgical wound(s) including blood loss, temperature changes, nutrition, mental status changes, and discharge plans."

What was Lynn's role on the morning rounds? "When the 'just-in-time' opportunities arose," she explains, "I educated the group about various electronic library resources available to them so they could use the medical literature to make safer patient care decisions based on evidence instead of Google. When asked or when I perceived a need, I performed MEDLINE searches on given topics and saved the searches for use in the future. I gave detailed instructions on how to run the searches and see the search strategies. When asked a direct question, I supplied a patient-filtered reply from a variety of knowledge-based resources within twenty-four hours to the patient care team, thus allowing them time to concentrate on their own responsibility—patient care."

During her seventeen years at UMDNJ, Lynn also attended patient care rounds in the Department of Medicine and the Department of Allergy, Immunology, and Rheumatology doing tasks similar to those stated above. She routinely taught classes on EndNote, a bibliographic software program, to interns and residents at the request of the director of medical education. In addition, she taught special sessions on finding and using evidence-based medicine research. She was listed as part-time instructor in the Department of Allergy, Immunology, and Rheumatology. In addition, Lynn took part in the noon interdisciplinary tumor conference, prepared handouts, and was the occasional guest speaker. "My presence at this meeting made it extremely convenient for the attendee who had informational needs or questions regarding library electronic services to get immediate answers," she says.

Lynn was also involved with the preparation of topic-specific article lists for the Department of Pediatrics for their weekly grand rounds conference. "I also participated in the hospital's Patient Education Committee for many years," she says. "I provided information about our electronic library resources or answered questions asked by the committee members that would benefit them in creating better patient education materials. One time I prepared a tri-fold handout on newborn HIV/AIDS testing given to new mothers. Another time I prepared a guide to the hospital TV channels that offered patient education programming."

Lynn's primary clientele are the various students and faculty from the five schools at the UMDNJ Newark Campus (Medicine, Dentistry, Public Health, School of Related Professions, and Nursing), hospital house staff (interns, residents, and fellows), and attendings. Her secondary clientele are prescreened visitors who have legitimate science, health science, or medical research needs from colleges, universities, or health care vocational programs, as well as those studying for licensing exams, attorneys, or paralegals.

Lynn utilizes technology for convenience and rapid transmission of information. "The library purchased a Pocket PC that I brought with me on patient care rounds," she says. "I was able to use point-of-care software to answer questions as they arose. I also use the laptop to teach groups in the conference rooms along with an LCD projector." She regularly contributes to the University Libraries *EndNote* blog, wiki, and RLIG (Reference Librarians Informatics Group), a subgroup of the University Libraries Staff Group offered via the university's portal.

Lynn's interest in librarianship was influenced by her elementary school librarian. "Ms. Bunny Todd was a wonderful role model," she recalls. "For storytime she sat in a rocking chair and had us sit on the floor in a semicircle by the windows. She made the library fun. Even at an early age I loved being asked questions by my classmates and then finding the answers; I likened it to building a jigsaw puzzle." In high school she worked as a Reference Room library page in the town library in Fairfield, Connecticut. "I had a wonderful boss who gave me increasingly difficult library clerk tasks to do so I could learn new skills," she says. "Outside of the Reference Room I shelved books, did shelf-reading, and processed new books with jackets and pockets."

She received her bachelor's degree in psychology and her M.L.S. degree (with a specialization in special libraries) from Southern Connecticut State College. During library school, she enrolled in a semester internship with Clairol, Inc., to gain some corporate work experience. "One of the weekly projects I was given was to prepare the company's print patent index by scanning the *Patent Gazette* for relevant products and—believe it or not—cutting and pasting the entries onto sheets of paper for reproduction. By doing so I learned primitive competitive intelligence. I was taught how to create computer strategies via Dialog, even though I could not execute the searches."

After library school, Lynn worked at a variety of companies such as Uniroyal Chemical, GE Corporate Legal, GE Corporate Business, Bristol Myers-Squibb, and the *Stamford Advocate* (a newspaper). She was a freelance librarian employed through a library placement agency. "Experience at these companies allowed me to better define my likes and dislikes," she says. "I learned that I loved the field of medicine, pharmaceutical sciences, and health, and that I disliked business." She worked as a cataloger/acquisitionist/reference librarian at Young and Rubicam headquarters, the third-largest advertising agency in the world, located on Madison Avenue in New York City. She loved the reference work but despised cataloging. "I held this position for a year before I was fired," she recounts. "I was devastated! In retrospect, it was a blessing in disguise because it presented me with an opportunity to look for a medical reference librarian position instead of remaining there unsatisfied."

She then took a position as hospital librarian at the Frederick M. Dearborn Medical Library in the Metropolitan Hospital Center, which is affiliated with the New York Medical College in Valhalla, New York. "I was the second-in-command at this four-person library," she says. "I did reference, bibliographic instruction, Ovid MEDLINE searching, and interacted with library patrons. I was told I had a very good rapport with library patrons, especially the house staff, and was told I made the library come alive. I was frequently asked clinical questions by the chief of the ER. There was even a time when he phoned me with a search request during an operation and I provided him with the needed information without panicking. That was an epiphany for me; I realized I loved answering clinical questions and wanted to do more. When an advertisement appeared in the Sunday *New York Times* Education section for a clinical librarian position at UMDNJ, I applied."

When Lynn first started in her current position at UMDNJ, she had to struggle for the right to attend morning report and patient rounds. "The chairman of the Department of Medicine believed that only medical students, residents, interns, fellows, attendings, and pharmacists should be present. My predecessor in the position never had the desire to participate in patient rounds, so my request initially faced resistance."

Eventually her request was granted, but she offers this caveat: "If the department chairs are not library advocates, your services will never be appreciated or utilized to their fullest."

To those interested in pursuing a career in clinical librarianship, Lynn stresses the importance of being a competent database searcher and being acquainted with the infrastructure and the personnel of a hospital and its affiliated university. "Being amenable to flexible hours is also very useful," she says. "Surgery meets at 6 o'clock in the morning and Ophthalmology meets at 7 p.m. This schedule was possible for me before I became the mother of twins! On the other hand, some clinical librarianship positions are part-time between several different hospitals, or a combination position—such as mine—of reference duties in the library and clinical duties in the hospital.

"Hospital department involvement varies greatly due to a number of factors, so expect change," she continues. "Just when you've learned medical terminology for a medical specialty, it's time to learn another! You might want to work for a specific department because you have an interest in that specialty, but if they don't want you there, you're out of luck. Also, you should expect that specialization will naturally occur on the job. My areas of specialization over the years have gone from AIDS research to alternatives in animal testing, simply due to my departmental involvement."

Lynn also says that it's important to be able to effectively teach library patrons without any assumptions about their skill levels. "Sometimes you have to start at square one," she explains. "One time I posted instructions in the Department of Medicine Resident's Lounge about how to get to the library home page . . . neglecting to include how to turn on the PC and printer!"

You also have to be very familiar with your collections, including print resources. "Being a librarian today still involves knowing the print collection; despite what our students think, all information is not gotten from the Web by doing a Google search! I can successfully answer patron questions even when the Internet goes down. It's also very important to me to teach patrons to evaluate information sources to find those that are current, authoritative, unbiased, and reputable.

"Please keep in mind that there are very few clinical librarian positions available because of funding," Lynn concludes. "But don't give up searching. It's worth the pursuit because the questions posed are interesting and challenging. There isn't a day that goes by when I don't learn something new."

STEPHANIE MIDKIFF

Associate Professor and Reference Librarian, John E. Jaqua Law Library,
University of Oregon, Eugene, Oregon

*"There are so many facets of law librarianship that anyone
can find a niche and make a difference."*

ONE MIGHT wonder why a person with a full-fledged law degree would even consider librarianship as a career. After going to law school, passing the bar exam, and
working as a lawyer in the field, what would drive someone to go to library school?
For Stephanie Midkiff, the answer was simple. "After seven years of working as an
attorney, I decided I wanted to branch out and do something else while still utilizing
my law degree," she says. "It is a decision that I have never regretted."

In her position as a law reference librarian at the University of Oregon's (UO) law
library, Stephanie's duties are varied. "Along with helping to staff the reference desk
several hours a week," she says, "I do classroom instruction, collection development,
and faculty support. We provide in-person, telephone, e-mail, and chat reference services to our patrons. Sometimes reference interactions lead to more in-depth research
and consultation, especially for law students and law faculty. I have written research
guides to help patrons navigate the process of legal research."

During the school year, Stephanie spends a good portion of her time working with
the Legal Research and Writing Program, providing editorial assistance for assignments, doing classroom instruction on online legal research in Westlaw and Lexis
(legal databases), and serving as a guest lecturer in advanced legal research courses as
well as other university courses at the request of faculty. "We librarians tailor our presentations to the content of the courses to make them more meaningful for students,"
she says. "We also do small group instruction to advise law students on resources for
independent research projects."

In addition, Stephanie is responsible for collection development in several different subject and curricular areas. "I have particular faculty that I work with to support
their scholarship, teaching, and research," she says. "I provide research assistance to
them as well as individualized training to their research assistants."

The law library at UO is integrated into the main UO Libraries System, and the
librarians have faculty rank without tenure. Stephanie is an associate professor and
is involved with committees and projects within the Libraries System. "We conduct
business in library faculty meetings," she says. "Contract renewal and promotion for
the librarians involves initial review by a library faculty personnel committee, subject

to approval by the dean of the libraries and the university provost." Librarians at UO are encouraged to become involved with other units on campus. Stephanie currently serves on a campus committee that reviews applicants for Fulbright scholarships and has represented the libraries on the University Senate.

"I also serve as the law library's liaison to the three student-run law journals at our law school and provide in-depth training to source-pullers for cite-checking articles," Stephanie says. "I meet with staff during journal orientation to familiarize them with library policies and the special services the law library extends to the journals.

"As a public institution, our law library and the print (and many electronic) collections are open to anyone," Stephanie explains. "However, our primary constituents are the law faculty and administration, and law students here at the University of Oregon School of Law. Secondary patrons are other faculty and students on campus. As time allows, we also serve attorneys and other public patrons, including self-represented litigants. Accordingly, most of our primary constituents are pursuing or already have advanced degrees, as do attorneys who come in to use our facilities. We occasionally have community college students, students pursuing paralegal certification, and high school students. For the public at large, many have much formal education while others have very little.

"Our law faculty are a congenial group, easy to work with, and usually know precisely what they want when seeking reference help for their scholarship, teaching, and research," she continues. "Self-represented litigants can pose a challenge because reference librarians cannot give legal advice or engage in the practice of law, and that is often difficult to get across to a public patron. And it often requires more time to explain some of the legal concepts to them and how the legal resources are used; many pick up the strange world of legal research surprisingly quickly, however."

Stephanie finds the most challenging feature of her job to be keeping up with technology. "It's also a challenge to keep up with the changing landscape of legal information as evidenced by the consolidation of the legal publishing industry and the complexities that flow from that," she says. "So many resources essential to the legal profession—primary authority such as case law, statutes, regulations, agency decisions, treaties; secondary authority such as treatises, law journal articles, attorney practice materials, international materials—are now becoming available online, and libraries are having to make tough fiscal choices to avoid duplication with print resources, while keeping our primary constituents comfortable with access. It used to be fairly simple to figure out what it means when a court has designated an opinion 'to be published,' but now lines are blurred when previously unpublished opinions are now available in databases or on the Internet."

To help keep up with changes in the profession, Stephanie subscribes to several law library electronic discussion groups associated with the American Association of Law Libraries (AALL) and its regional chapter. She receives collection development alerts for new publications, and she monitors newsletters and news articles. "The UO Libraries System has an intranet with quite a few wikis that are used to organize and disseminate information and archive policies and procedures," she says. "The law library has a wiki with several categories of information. We also have a separate law intranet which we use to record meeting minutes and to make documents, information, and spreadsheets available to the rest of the law library staff."

Stephanie attends webinars and training events offered within the campus Libraries System. She is a member of AALL, the main professional association for law librarians, as well as WestPac (the Western Pacific Chapter of AALL), and remains active by serving on committees and elected positions. She attends the annual AALL meetings as well as the annual WestPac meetings. "Last year I attended the Online Northwest conference, which focuses on the use of technology within libraries generally, and found that very helpful and enjoyable," she says. "My institution is fairly generous in supporting travel to professional meetings, and this works out to funding for about two major meetings a year—one on the national level and one regionally."

The idea of becoming a law librarian didn't crop up until Stephanie had been working as an attorney for several years. She received her undergraduate degree in English from the University of Kentucky (UK) in Lexington and enrolled in law school several years later. "I graduated from the UK College of Law in 1985 and obtained my first job with Legal Services in rural Kentucky," she says. "After a year I began working for the Kentucky Court of Appeals as a staff attorney for various judges and as a criminal motions attorney on the central staff for the court. After about seven years I decided I wanted to branch out and do something else while still utilizing my law degree. I was mulling this over with a couple of old friends who had switched careers to librarianship, and they both said that it had been a great move and that they could imagine I would enjoy the profession also. So almost spur of the moment, I looked into getting into the library science program at UK, took the GRE (which I thought was ludicrous to be required to take, having passed the bar exam), and was admitted to the program beginning January 1994. Just prior to enrolling, my husband and I were living in Paducah in western Kentucky, and we sold our house and he moved into a small apartment while I rented a room in Lexington to start school. Because we were living apart, my goal was to finish the program as quickly as possible, so I went through the summer and finished in December 1994."

Stephanie is an associate member of the American Bar Association. She says that having the J.D. (juris doctorate) degree is generally required in order to be a reference librarian in an academic law library. "However, it is often not required if you work in other law library settings," she adds, "such as law firms, county law libraries, or other government law libraries."

She has some solid advice for those interested in a career in law librarianship. "I have had several opportunities in the last few years to talk with law students and others about careers in law librarianship," she says. "Without hesitation, I tell them that I think they will thoroughly enjoy it as a profession, that it is a decision they will never regret, a profession with a high degree of job satisfaction. There are so many facets of law librarianship available that you can find a niche where you fit in and can make a difference. Take advantage of courses in library management and courses that will put you in a good position regarding technology. Anyone entering the field of librarianship today cannot escape the pervasiveness of technology in the profession. You want to be as prepared as possible. We must all continue to hone our technological skills throughout our working lives. Also, take advantage of any opportunity to work in the type of library you think you are interested in. I felt it was a real drawback for my getting that first library job because I had no library work experience prior to enrolling in library science school, where I interned in the special library, medical library, and law library. Try to attend a program that has a concentration in the types of libraries you might be interested in. For instance, the AALL Recruitment to Law Librarianship Committee has an excellent website with loads of information, especially the site listing the various ALA-accredited graduate programs with specific classes in law librarianship.

"While in library science school, get involved in student chapters of professional associations. That is often a great way to connect with professionals and to network. Try to attend some professional meetings and take advantage of any career services provided such as interviewing during the conference. I have been doing this job for almost twelve years and have never regretted the decision," Stephanie concludes. "It's interesting, intellectually stimulating, entertaining, and you get to work with great colleagues."

Stephanie recommends the following websites:

- www.aallnet.org (American Association of Law Libraries)
- www.aallnet.org/committee/rllc/index.asp (AALL Recruitment to Law Librarianship Committee)

PETER SPRENKLE

Adult Reference Librarian, Waukegan Public Library, Waukegan, Illinois

"My personal motto at the reference desk is 'Leave no patron empty-handed.'"

PETER SPRENKLE is a reference librarian at the Waukegan Public Library. Throughout the years, he has had firsthand experience at answering questions from people in all walks of life—from children to the elderly—and has basically "seen it all." It's very likely that there isn't a question, no matter how bizarre, that Peter hasn't heard before. Here are a few examples: "Where can I get my birth certificate?" "How can I contain the bees in my backyard?" "How do you use a mouse?" "How do I save this document?" "Where is my library card?" "Does Venus have a ring around it?" "Was the *Dune* trilogy originally intended to be a trilogy?" "What were the names of the battleships used for heavy bombardment in the Battle of Saipan?" "My wife is in prison. What is the county clerk's phone number?"

All of the above questions were pulled from a blog that Peter created in 2003 called *Ref Grunt* (http://refgrunt.blogspot.com), in which he listed nearly every question and desk transaction that came his way for several years. The blog boasts a banner that reads, "Some days I love working the reference desk, some days I hate it, and it's often the same day." The posts clearly demonstrate how Peter's innate sense of humor helps carry him through even the most mundane and annoying of transactions. *"Ref Grunt* is my most famous web-based work," Peter says. "I started it anonymously as a way to blow off frustration at the desk." When he coauthored a book with Charles Anderson entitled *Reference Librarianship: Notes from the Trenches* (Routledge, 2006), his anonymity with the *Ref Grunt* blog was taken away. The book is similar to the blog in that it documents the daily professional life of a young librarian working "in the trenches" at a public library in the midwestern United States. "Coauthoring a book with Charles Anderson didn't help my anonymity at all," he says. "Now everyone knows about the blog, but I'm happy to say that no one at the library objects. The blog is retired, but I think people still read it. I'm posting the reference questions on Twitter now."

Peter spends much of his day "on call" for difficult reference questions. While the circulation staff handle the simple questions, such as how to work the copier, the more complex questions are directed to the reference librarians. "At 3 p.m., I come out of my office and more or less roam the place," he explains. "When not roaming, I primarily do collection management for the 600s, 700s, 800s, 900s, biographies, music

CDs, the Spanish language collection, and the adult and children's graphic novels. I also assist with virtual reference, and I cover any questions that come in through e-mail. Waukegan is a working-class community with a sizable African-American and Hispanic presence. The library is right next door to the Lake County Courthouse, so we get a lot of lawyers and jury members visiting as well."

Peter finds that answering reference questions is the most exciting feature of his job. "I think it becomes a point of honor to help the patron to the extent that they need," he says. "Coupled with that is the fact that the patrons often don't know what they need! We deal with technological issues as well, like saving a patron's document when they don't have a disk to save on, or figuring out why their photo is printing funny. Being able to help the patron get to where they expected to be is one of the most rewarding things I can think of. My personal motto is 'Leave no patron empty-handed.' Even if I can't solve their problem, I point them to someone, some organization, who can. I try to give them at least one thing to be hopeful about."

A self-proclaimed "computer nut," Peter began his career when the Internet was in its infancy. "At that time, no one knew what the Internet was," he says. "A few years later I was instrumental in creating the library's first web page—without telling the administration. A coworker and I attended an HTML seminar run by the North Suburban Library Service (NSLS) and then we returned to the library saying, 'Hey! The library has a web page!' We had mentioned web pages before but no one really understood what we were talking about when we asked them for content. After the page was up, however, they started coming to us and saying, 'Why don't you have my department's policies up there?'" Peter was also one of the library's early advocates of virtual reference. "I've been handling e-mail reference questions for a while," he says, "and now we not only contribute to AskAway, but we use IM (instant messaging) tools such as Meebo to give us additional points of access."

Like many others in the field, Peter stumbled into librarianship by virtue of the various library jobs he took to support himself while in school and immediately afterward. While studying music and theater at the University of Texas at Austin, he worked part-time shelving and copying items for the Texas Medical Association Library. "I moved to other positions at the university until I graduated," he says. "I wasn't sure what to do next, so I moved back to Urbana, my hometown, where I found myself working as an assistant in more libraries. I liked the work, and the peace and quiet, I think. I graduated in 1991 and got a position at Waukegan Public Library. I think they initially hired me because they needed someone with a music background to beef up the CD collection. My basic reference background was solid enough, but I got this job due to my background in music."

To keep up with changes in technology and the profession, Peter attends NSLS seminars, reads professional journals, and does a lot of "trial and error." He is a member of the American Library Association and the Illinois Library Association. He finds changes in technology to be exciting and has noticed that patron behavior changes as technology advances. "Patrons rarely ask us to look up addresses or phone numbers anymore," he says. "At the same time, more sophisticated catalogs have given us better ways to examine our collection usage."

If you are interested in reference work at a public library, Peter says, "besides being familiar with reference tools—whether in print or online—you need a basic knowledge of how software works. At our library, that means Windows, Office, etc. By 'basic' I mean just that. An amazing number of patrons come in without a concept of saving their work, and many others don't realize how important that is. Others don't know how to save onto their thumb drives, or need someone to show them how to upload pictures or documents that they have saved. Sometimes drives or computers are defective, so we have to learn to work around that. Some basic word-processing knowledge helps us as well, such as spacing and setting margins. Also, don't forget to learn about the old print sources. At the same time, keep an eye out for the latest technology. Your arsenal can never be too big.

"Some patrons have never been exposed to database searching before, and they need instruction," Peter continues. "They are often quite surprised that such databases exist and that there is still a ton of information out there that's not available in Google. When we do get more advanced patrons, they often need guidance on how to use the subscription databases we offer."

This brings up a question that Peter has encountered before: "Why do we need reference librarians in public libraries when we have Google and Wikipedia?" He is ready with his answer. "It is important for the uninitiated, naive researcher to learn that multiple sources must be used. It's also important to show them how to find these sources. You might say, 'that's what Google is for,' and indeed Google is an excellent research tool to start with. But left to their own devices, these naive researchers are likely to dump words in the search box and see what they get. They still need training, not only on how to create an effective Boolean search using the filters they may not even know Google's got, but on how to judge the validity of the results.

"Showing patrons how to do research at least a little better is one of our responsibilities," Peter concludes. "That will not change anytime soon."

Note: As of August 2009, Peter no longer works at Waukegan Public Library and is pursuing Teaching English as a Foreign Language.

ELIZABETH B. KUDWA

Business Librarian, Capital Area District Library, Lansing, Michigan

"Strong reference skills are a must for a business librarian.
It also doesn't hurt to be naturally curious."

IF YOU are a librarian with a strong business and marketing background and you enjoy doing research, but a corporate environment does not appeal to you, what are the professional options? One option would be to look for a business reference position in a large public library system, where you could continue doing what you enjoy without the stress of tight deadlines. This is exactly what Elizabeth Kudwa set out to find and was happily successful.

Elizabeth has a bachelor's degree in business administration with a concentration in marketing from the University of Michigan at Flint. Before becoming a librarian, she worked at a marketing research/consulting firm. "I really enjoyed the research aspect of my job as an analyst," she says, "but I did not enjoy the tight demands placed on us by our clients. I decided to begin looking for a career where I could continue doing research but where I wouldn't be under so many tight deadlines and stress. I came across the field of librarianship and thought it was a perfect fit." Her plan was to become a corporate librarian, but she soon changed her mind when she realized the trend in big companies was to cut librarians during budget crises. Instead, she decided to focus on public libraries.

After earning her master's degree in library science from Wayne State University, Elizabeth took a part-time job in the children's department of a medium-sized public library. "I didn't really think I'd find a business librarian position in a public library," she says. "Fortunately for me, the district library located in our state's capital is big enough to have a need for that type of position. I was hired as the business librarian for the Capital Area District Library in Lansing. I am the first business librarian my district has ever hired.

"My position has evolved quite a bit over the last six years," Elizabeth says. When she first started out, she was responsible for all aspects of business: personal finance, investing, careers/employment, small business, and so on. When economic conditions declined in the state of Michigan, the focus of the business librarian position switched to small businesses and entrepreneurs. "It was felt that we could do the most good for the community we serve by concentrating on helping small businesses get started and grow," she explains.

Elizabeth provides business reference services to anyone who is considering starting a business or who is in the process of starting a business. She also helps existing business owners with market research. She is responsible for creating and maintaining various resources for small business patrons. "This includes creating small business resource guides to help patrons more easily find the materials they need," she explains. "It also involves creating and updating content on the business portion of our website (www.cadl.org/answers/business/) and working with the head of reference to select and purchase business reference materials and databases."

Entrepreneurs and small business owners can make appointments with Elizabeth for research assistance and consulting. "I may use this time to teach someone how to use a database, or to talk through what their specific research needs are," she says. "Sometimes I walk them through the Business Reference section so they can see what resources we have available. Most of the time people want answers to market research questions in order to complete a business plan."

Elizabeth is also involved with outreach to the small business community. She attends meetings of the chambers of commerce and the local business associations and often finds herself volunteering for service on a committee with one of these groups. "Sometimes I am asked to be a guest speaker," she says, "in which case I talk about the business services and resources available through our library." Two times per year she offers workshops for small business owners on topics such as how to write a business plan and how to optimize a website to get more traffic.

"This year we are running a business plan–writing contest for the first time," Elizabeth says. "All applicants are required to attend four workshops designed to help them write their plan: Writing a Business Plan, Market Research, Marketing Your Business, and Small Business Financials." She also runs a monthly entrepreneur club called "Start It Up" at one of the branch libraries. The club has generated a lot of discussion and networking opportunities for participants.

Twice monthly, Elizabeth submits articles for a regular column that she writes in the community's multicultural newspaper, *The New Citizens Press*. The column, called "Ask the Business Librarian," focuses on various business topics. Some of her recent articles have discussed writing successful résumés, naming a new business, blogging to promote a business, and social networking for small business owners.

Elizabeth says that the most challenging part of her job involves trying to make the best of the resources the library can afford to purchase. "Many of the business databases available today are quite expensive," she says, "and for a public library it's just not practical to purchase subscriptions to multiple business databases. We do quite well with what we have and I always keep my eye on tailoring our business offerings as much as we can. But there are occasions when I need to refer patrons to the university library because they have more business resources than we do.

"The most exciting part of my job is working with entrepreneurs," Elizabeth continues. "You will not find people more passionate about what they do. That enthusiasm is contagious. Entrepreneurs that are truly serious about starting a business are some of the most interesting people I have ever met, and it's very exciting to help them work through their research and see something very positive come out of that."

Technology plays a big part in helping Elizabeth stay up-to-date. To keep in touch with other business librarians, Elizabeth uses chat tools such as Google Chat as well as collaboration tools like Google Docs, wikis, and blogs. "I talk regularly online with colleagues in other parts of the state," she says. "Without tools to facilitate immediate discussions online, we wouldn't be able to share ideas as easily or as often." She subscribes to various RSS feeds (*Business Week, Fast Company,* and the *Economist*) and to various business blogs (*Small Business Trends, Duct Tape Marketing, Business Pundit, Entrepreneur,* and the *Inc.* magazine blog). "Having headlines and various articles sent to me is really helpful for staying on top of what's happening in small business."

Elizabeth reads several professional journals such as *ONLINE, Unabashed Librarian,* and *Reference Reviews,* as well as several business publications such as *Inc.* magazine, *Entrepreneur, Fast Company,* and *Business Week.* She also takes continuing education courses and attends annual conferences. She is a member of the Michigan Library Association and the American Library Association. Within the ALA, she is a member of the Reference and User Services Association and the Business Reference and Services Section.

To those interested in becoming business librarians, Elizabeth says, "Strong reference skills are a must. This includes everything from conducting a thorough reference interview to being able to knowledgeably use various business resources to answer patron questions. It also doesn't hurt to be naturally curious." In library school, she took courses in business reference and in government documents, both of which turned out to be directly applicable to her current position. She also had a practicum in a corporate bank library during her last term.

"In addition to the M.L.I.S., I would suggest considering a business degree—either a B.B.A. or an M.B.A.," she says. "Having that business background only makes the job that much easier and lends much more credibility to the service you provide. There are a lot of advantages to being something of a specialist in a certain subject, like business. It allows the librarian to help the patron a great deal, and can make for a more satisfying patron experience. It also helps the librarian to build a good collection of relevant resources.

"Another piece of advice would be to learn how to network effectively. Librarians—and this is a generalization—tend to be somewhat introverted. It can be hard for them to get out from behind the reference desk and go out into the community. But if you are going to be a successful business librarian, you have to be able to do that. Learning how to network effectively will give you confidence and make it easier for you to get out into the community.

"Being a librarian today means something entirely different than it did even five or ten years ago," Elizabeth says. "I've been a practicing librarian for six years and have seen some definite changes. Colleagues that have been in the profession longer also comment regularly on just how much things have changed. The changes all seem to revolve around electronic resources. Print reference collections are being scaled down and replaced with either databases or electronic books. Working with patrons to help them realize that their favorite resources are still available, just in a different format, has been challenging. Not all patrons embrace the electronic world. We have to work hard to educate our users to make sure they can find and use these new electronic resources."

Elizabeth says that the following are the top five websites she can't live without (in no particular order):

- http://factfinder.census.gov (U.S. Census Bureau)
- http://smallbiztrends.com (Small Business Trends)
- www.ducttapemarketing.com/blog/ (*Duct Tape Marketing* blog)
- www.inc.com (*Inc.*, a magazine for the small business owner)
- www.entrepreneur.com (*Entrepreneur*, a magazine for the small business owner)

VICKI F. CROFT

Head, Animal Health Library, Washington State University, Pullman, Washington

"Veterinary librarians are a rare breed."

"WHAT IS the jaw grip strength of a pit bull?" "Which animals have cleaner mouths—dogs or cats?" "Where can I find information on MRSA infections in veterinary hospitals?" "Where can I find information on DNA fingerprinting for llamas? I'm involved in a paternity suit; a male llama jumped the fence, and paternity is in question." If these questions sound surreal to you, they are in fact run-of-the-mill reference questions for Vicki Croft. She is a member of that "rare breed"—a very small group of librarians with a unique specialization in veterinary medical librarianship.

As head of the Animal Health Library at Washington State University (WSU), Vicki is responsible for the management of the library and its services. She selects and purchases books to support the teaching, learning, and research needs of the primary library users—the faculty, staff, and students of the College of Veterinary Medicine (CVM). She answers reference questions in person, by phone, fax, or e-mail from WSU personnel as well as practicing veterinarians, pet owners, breeders, lawyers, or anyone in need of animal health information. In addition, she gives lectures on library use to classes, groups, and individuals as requested, and participates in instructional programs such as the CVM's award-winning "Diagnostic Challenges" in which veterinary student teams work on cases with "clients" under the supervision of a veterinary faculty member. "The 'client' is someone who poses as an owner of an animal with a disease," Vicki explains. "The student team must successfully diagnose and develop a care plan for the client's animal. Library use is required, as students must do a literature search during the case. These cases used in the Diagnostic Challenges are taken from cases seen by the WSU Veterinary Teaching Hospital and veterinarians in private practices.

"A great deal of research is conducted by faculty and students," says Vicki, "and that requires access to journals and books in a wide variety of fields, from cardiology to immunology, microbiology, orthopedics, anesthesia, and the like. I meet with new faculty, including residents and interns, as well as graduate and professional students. The staff and I locally manage circulation, reference, and interlibrary loan services. (Our main campus library does our purchasing, serials, binding, cataloging, and other central services.) I attend library-wide meetings as an administrator and unit head. I also attend some committee meetings in the CVM, such as the Safety Committee."

The primary clientele of the Animal Health Library are the faculty, including interns, residents, and other house officers, staff, and the graduate and professional students of the CVM. Besides veterinary medicine, the CVM includes the Programs in Neurosciences, the Washington Animal Disease Diagnostic Laboratory, the Food Animal Investigational Unit, the School for Global Animal Health (http://globalhealth .wsu.edu), and the School of Molecular Biosciences. "In addition to the teaching role of veterinary schools, research and extension functions are very important," Vicki says. "WSU CVM researchers receive a significant number of dollars in research funding from agencies such as the National Institutes of Health and the U.S. Agricultural Research Services, as well as animal health companies and foundations, such as the Morris Animal Foundation. Veterinary, medical, and basic science research journals are essential to the research and teaching needs of the veterinary faculty, staff, and students. We also support researchers who do literature searches in order to meet the requirements of the Animal Welfare Act, before the researchers' grants can be submitted and funded. Animal testing and alternatives to animal use, animal welfare and experimentation, and human-animal bonding and interactions are other subjects of interest to users of veterinary libraries such as mine.

"Veterinary libraries are unique," Vicki says. "Unlike medical or hospital libraries, our 'patients' are many species ranging from cats and dogs and birds, hamsters, and other exotics such as hedgehogs—to farm and food animals such as cattle, sheep, goats, llamas—to wildlife and zoo animals such as bighorn sheep, elk, deer, camels, cougars, elephants, tigers, and giraffes. Our library users need books and journals to support all species and all medical specialties, including human medicine. Animal medicine borrows from human medicine, and human medicine borrows from veterinary medicine. Animal models of human disease are important research tools in helping to diagnose, treat, and cure human diseases. Examples from the past include diabetes and leprosy. Veterinary medicine borrows from human medicine in utilizing medical tools, procedures, and instruments, such as CAT, MRI, laparoscopy, and more. For instance, the first CAT and MRI in our university town were in the College of Veterinary Medicine. For a number of years the CVM's MRI was used by our local hospital, as well as the veterinary school—humans in the mornings, animals in the afternoons!"

Vicki says that the specialty of veterinary medical librarianship is different from any other because in order to do the job well, one must draw upon resources in human medicine, zoology, and the basic sciences such as physiology, cell biology, and anatomy, as well as some agricultural components such as animal science, reproduction, and nutrition. "Business and practice management are necessary, too," she says. "Public health has become increasingly important because of zoonotic diseases such as avian influenza, toxoplasmosis, West Nile fever, ebola, and more. The concept of 'one health initiative' is becoming increasingly important due to the growing recognition of the effect of animal health on human health and quality of life globally. This brought about the recent founding of WSU's School for Global Animal Health.

"There are only 28 schools of veterinary medicine in the United States and 5 in Canada," says Vicki. "Most veterinary librarians work in these libraries. There are very few who work for veterinary drug companies and nutrition. Medical school and drug company librarians who deal with researchers who work with laboratory animals used in testing have interests in common with veterinary librarians, too. Other animal health-related librarians include zoo, wildlife, aquarium, and primate center librarians. However, animal health is only one component of their subject area. For example, areas of interest to zoo librarians include animal husbandry, breeding reproduction, and nutrition, as well as zoo management, visitor information, public relations, etc.

"Because veterinary medical librarianship is such a small, cohesive group, it is possible to personally know all of our colleagues in the nation," Vicki says. "This is in contrast with other health information professionals, such as hospital librarians, who number in the thousands." Vicki keeps in close touch with her colleagues through several electronic discussion lists such as VETLIB-L (Veterinary Medicine library issues and information) and HLIB-NW (Health Library-Northwest). "Electronic discussion lists are my lifeline and connection to veterinary library colleagues throughout the world," she says. "They help me with my job, in providing information about new services and functions, in answering reference questions, obtaining photocopies of articles needed urgently, preparing and planning for meetings, sharing information and asking questions of colleagues about special problems, and work on special projects."

Vicki finds it challenging to keep up with technology and adapt to user needs. To face that challenge head-on, she stays involved with social networks and tools. She follows blogs, belongs to Facebook (there are Facebook groups for veterinary and medical librarians), creates and maintains a delicious site for the library (http://www.delicious.com/wsuhsl), maintains an e-mail reference request form, and is starting to use Meebo to communicate problems to the library systems office and for reference use. "I have also helped create two major collections for the WSU Research Exchange, WSU's institutional repository," she says. "The first is an open-access, full-text repository of the papers presented at the first five International Conferences for Animal Health Information Specialists. The second is a comprehensive bibliography entitled Animal Health Libraries, Librarians, and Librarianship: A Bibliography. It now includes more than 900 references, with hot links when available. I plan to continue to maintain both collections, even beyond retirement."

Vicki recalls that when she first graduated from library school, technology was only beginning to transform and influence library operations, mainly in technical services. She has been witness to many technological changes throughout her years as a librarian. She has seen databases move from print format to mediated searching on CD-ROM, and finally to end-user remote Internet access. She has seen collections move from print to online. At the start of her career, communication with colleagues began with letters that were mailed, then moved to phone calls, then fax, then e-mail, then Skype and teleconferencing. Photocopying of journal articles has morphed into scanning and electronic delivery. Heavy use of print books and journals has all but disappeared. She has witnessed decreasing gate counts as more and more people make use of remote access. She has had to justify space for books and other printed materials against other institutional space priorities. She has watched as student study preference shifted from using study carrels and large tables in an environment of "silence" to small group tables, small group study rooms, and conference rooms where eating, drinking, and group discussions are sanctioned.

"Today the emergence of e-journals has had the greatest effect on the way academic libraries operate," says Vicki. "Troubleshooting e-journal problems is a frequent need. Decisions on print versus electronic, to bind or not, bundled e-journal vendor packages, etc., are necessary. Due to remote access and decreasing gate counts, we need to find other ways to reach library users, particularly those who now see little need to visit the physical library. We find ourselves retooling libraries into student-centered, collaborative areas where print and electronic resources are used in tandem for group and special projects. When the Internet goes down or the lights go off, we are left feeling helpless!"

Vicki had always been enthralled with libraries and books, and the idea of becoming a librarian emerged while she was working on her B.S. in biology at Dana College, a small midwestern liberal arts college. In college she worked in the biology lab and as a student assistant in the library. Her advisor brought to her attention a medical librarianship trainee program with the U.S. Public Health Services, which would take advantage of her biology background and her interest in and experience with libraries. She applied to several schools that offered the program and ultimately selected the University of Illinois. "It was a really good deal," she says, "because not only did it pay for my tuition plus some living expenses, but also provided training in a field that most interested me—science and medical librarianship." The program lasted fifteen months, and she took courses in science, medical reference, and materials selection, and completed an internship with a faculty member doing research on animal physiology.

Her first professional position was as a science librarian at the University of Nebraska at Lincoln. She worked with its five branches, including the Chemistry, Geology, and Life Sciences Libraries. She was there for five years before accepting the position of head of the Veterinary Medical Library at Washington State University, where she made several moves into increasingly challenging positions and responsibilities. After three years, the library assumed responsibility for the College of Pharmacy collections and services and was renamed the Veterinary Medical/Pharmacy Library. Later, more medical collections were added and the name changed again to the Health Sciences Library. Finally, the library settled into the entity that it is today—the Animal Health Library.

Vicki is a member of the Medical Library Association, including the Veterinary Medical Libraries Section, the International Cooperation Section, and the Pacific Northwest Chapter. She is a distinguished member of the MLA's professional development and career recognition program called the Academy of Health Information Professionals and feels that this sort of peer-reviewed certification is important to the profession. She is also a member of the Evidence-Based Veterinary Medical Association, the U.S. Agricultural Information Network (USAIN), and the Inland Northwest Health Science Libraries Consortium. "I feel that participation in veterinary and medical local, regional, national, and international library associations is very important," she says. "Involvement with agricultural librarian groups such as USAIN is also quite valuable." She attends professional conferences to keep up with technology as well as to network with colleagues. "Networking with my fellow veterinary librarians is an extremely important and valuable part of my job," she says. This connection with colleagues often results in collaborative national and international projects that she finds rewarding.

To those interested in veterinary librarianship, Vicki says that subject interest or a background in the sciences are assets but are not mandatory. "What is necessary is an understanding of scientific and medical literature and research, as well as literature needs of researchers and how they use the materials." She says that computer skills are a must, as are teaching skills and a willingness to learn new things. The ability to multitask is important, as well as the qualities of flexibility, adaptability "from species to species and back to human," creativity, innovation, and the ability to manage and administer services and personnel.

When Vicki first decided to become a librarian, she never dreamed what a rewarding career she would have. "During my career I've traveled to more than twenty countries on five continents to visit veterinary libraries," Vicki says. "I have friends all over the world and have longtime friendships that have lasted 25–30 years. My most rewarding activity as a veterinary librarian was serving as one of the founders of the International Conferences of Animal Health Information Specialists (ICAHIS). The very first meeting held in Reading, England, had eighty participants from eighteen countries. Subsequent meetings have been held in London, Copenhagen, Budapest, Ondersteport (South Africa), and Brisbane." She is now involved in planning for the seventh ICAHIS, to be held in Boston, in conjunction with the eleventh International Congress on Medical Librarianship and the 2013 annual MLA meeting. "The meetings provide an avenue for me to meet librarians from all over the world and many countries," she says.

Satisfying experiences occur in the library as well. "We once had a veterinary cardiologist who urgently needed an article in a journal that had not yet arrived at the library and was not available online," she recounts. "His patient (a client's dog) was in pre-op waiting to go into heart surgery. We called a veterinary librarian colleague at the University of Missouri who faxed us the article within ten minutes. The cardiologist rushed back to the OR with the article in hand. The next day, a box of chocolates was delivered to the library with this note: 'Your dedicated service above and beyond the call of duty is greatly appreciated. The reference article you obtained aided in the positive diagnosis and subsequent surgical repair of a puppy's congenital heart defect. The puppy is now at home and doing well.' What could be more rewarding than that?"

Vicki recommends the following websites:

- http://listserv.vt.edu/cgi-bin/wa?A0=vetlib-l (Veterinary Medicine Library issues and information electronic discussion list)
- www.vmls.mlanet.org (Veterinary Medical Libraries Section of the Medical Library Association)
- http://hdl.handle.net/2376/1469 (Animal Health Libraries, Librarians, and Librarianship: A Bibliography)
- https://research.wsulibs.wsu.edu:8443/dspace/handle/2376/1376/ (the International Conferences of Animal Health Information Specialists, Proceedings, 1992–)
- http://mlanet.org/academy/index.html (the Medical Library Association's Academy of Health Information Professionals)

DOLORES ZEGAR JUDKINS

Head, Information, Research, and Outreach Department,
Oregon Health and Science University Library, Portland, Oregon

*"In the health care field, finding the correct
information could be a matter of life and death."*

Despite the abundance of resources now available to the general consumer, finding appropriate and reliable health information is becoming more and more difficult. This particular challenge is one that Dolores Judkins, as a medical librarian, faces on a daily basis. It is also a source of great excitement for her.

As the head of the Information, Research, and Outreach Department at Oregon Health and Science University (OHSU) Library, a large part of Dolores's job is to help students, faculty, and the general public connect with medical information. "The level of service given to any one person can be anything from simply finding an article or a book on a topic to doing in-depth research," she says. "We may spend hours working on a MEDLINE search or finding specific information. We also do a lot of on-the-spot training with students, not only helping them find the information they need, but also helping them learn how to use various resources and introducing them to resources they may not know about."

Dolores says part of what makes her job interesting is that, apart from very basic questions, she has never had the same question twice. "There may be different aspects of a topic, but it's never exactly the same," she explains. "It's always thrilling when the person I'm working with gets excited about learning about new resources or finding the exact information they need. Every time someone says I've just made their lives easier makes it a good day for me. It's exciting to me to open up a whole new world of information for people who have no idea that it's out there."

Dolores says that expert searching is essential when dealing with medical information. "Finding information is easy with Google and Wikipedia," Dolores says. "However, finding the *best* information is *not* easy, and takes skill and expertise. I don't believe I've ever answered a hard question without wondering what else I might have missed. In the health field it's particularly important, when it really could mean the difference between life and death. Knowing all the ins and outs of a database, using controlled vocabularies and Boolean logic, are all skills that need practice. Finding 25 very good articles on a topic is far superior to finding 250,000 web pages on a topic.

"Librarians have now become teachers," Dolores continues. "Sure there's Google, but learning how to negotiate Google and other databases or search engines to find the best information is a skill that librarians can pass on to their patrons. Expert searching includes thinking beforehand about the best places to find the information. Rarely do I use only one resource. Moving from one resource to another presents different facets of an answer. Reference librarians are still needed to do the hard, in-depth searching, to help others learn how to search more effectively, and to guide others to the correct resources."

Dolores is responsible for five librarians and one library technician. Besides general departmental administration duties such as budget, staff evaluation, and hiring, she is also part of the Collection Development Committee and does general reference work such as bibliographic searching, reference desk staffing, and instruction. The library's primary clientele are OHSU students, staff, and faculty. One of the services offered to faculty, and for which Dolores is responsible, is the Library Liaison Program. This program "provides a platform for dialogue between the library and OHSU schools, departments, and programs in order to enhance the library's understanding of user needs and to promote the library's services and resources." Each of OHSU's librarians is liaison to one or more departments at the university. Liaison activities include periodic meetings with departments to relay updates on library services; tailoring specific classes for the department; providing assistance on research needs; orientations of new faculty and staff; designing a library portal for the department; and requesting information on specific resource needs from the department. As liaison coordinator, Dolores is kept quite busy.

"My daily work schedule varies, but generally includes meetings, reference duties, and teaching," says Dolores. "There are never two days alike, it seems. A lot of my time is spent dealing with e-mail."

Dolores says that technology plays a huge part in her job. She uses MEDLINE, a biomedical bibliographic database, on an almost constant basis. "MEDLINE was one of the very first computerized databases, putting medical libraries on the cutting edge," she says. "I have been searching MEDLINE since 1977, in a variety of formats, so doing searches for others—or teaching others how to search—has always been a large part of my job. The ability to find good answers to clinical questions is a vital skill, and indexed online databases, such as MEDLINE, make it much easier than paper indexes. Also, e-mail and online journals and books make it much easier to get the information to those who need it quickly."

Dolores uses blogs, wikis, and social software such as Facebook to keep up with what is happening in the field of medical librarianship. "I subscribe to blogs on evidence-based medicine in libraries, medical reference, and others," she says. "We use a blog at work to communicate among departments. I also keep up with changing technology by attending conferences, reading the literature, talking to other librarians, and taking continuing education classes. It's never-ending, but always interesting."

She is a member of the Medical Library Association and is a distinguished member of the MLA's credentialing society called the Academy of Health Information Professionals. She is also a member of the American Library Association, the Association of College and Research Libraries, and her regional chapter of the MLA. "The medical librarianship field is a very tight and supportive group," she says, "possibly because many medical librarians work in hospitals where they are solo librarians. Having a connection to other librarians through technology is very important; it's like having virtual colleagues. I do believe that if you are a member of a professional organization, you should participate in some way—as an officer, on a committee, or attending meetings."

Having loved libraries her entire life, Dolores considered librarianship as a career fairly early on. While earning her B.A. in sociology from Portland State University, she worked as a student library assistant. After graduation she joined VISTA (Volunteers in Service to America; now called AmeriCorps). "I considered social work until my VISTA experiences convinced me that I was not cut out for that," she says. "I applied for library school and was lucky to receive a fellowship award at the University of Oregon for a Community College Library fellowship program, which meant that my education and living expenses were covered for my year of library school. After I received my M.L.S. I joined the Peace Corps where I set up the first public library in Honduras. Since then I've worked in public libraries, special libraries, and health sciences libraries (both hospital and academic)."

Once she became a medical librarian, Dolores took a course on medical terminology. She continues to take continuing education classes on different aspects of medical librarianship. To those interested in a similar career, she says, "You have to always want to learn new things and have knowledge of what is on the horizon. Even though you may not use a particular technology, you need to know what it is and how it's used. You have to hire good people who are interested in always learning as well. You have to want to help people find the information they need, and you have to be able to pass on to them the desire to get the best information available."

Dolores says that being a librarian today is very different from when she first became one. "At that point, computers were not a part of a librarian's daily work. Although our goal has always been to find the best answer to a question, today we can find more and better information much more quickly using technology. Librarians have had to change with the times, continually learning as newer technologies become available. I believe that the use of technology in libraries has made the field more attractive to many people. The old image of the librarian searching through books has been changed to librarians spending more time teaching, helping with online research, and designing online guides to make research easier. I suspect that if there had not been such huge changes in librarianship over the years, I would have looked for another career after a while. The fact that I have had to continue learning new things and doing new things has kept this profession interesting to me."

If you are considering becoming a librarian, Dolores says, "Do it! I have been a librarian for over thirty years, and I still love it. If you like to find answers, it is the job for you. Spend some time working in a library before you go to library school if you can; it will help you make up your mind if that's what you really want. If you intend to work in a specialized library, such as a medical or science library, take some classes in those fields so that you understand the discipline. Librarianship is fun. Every day brings a new question that can test our skills and knowledge. Although there are days I wish everything would stop to let me catch up, I'm always interested in what research tool might be just around the corner."

Dolores recommends the following websites:

- www.mlanet.org/resources/expert_search/ (Medical Library Association Resources: Expert Searching)
- http://pss.mlanet.org/mailman/listinfo/expertsearching_pss.mlanet.org (Expert Searching electronic discussion list registration)
- http://ebmlibrarian.wetpaint.com (*Evidence-Based Medicine Librarian* blog)

DAVID BIGWOOD

Assistant Manager for Library Services, Lunar and Planetary Institute, Houston, Texas

"Like Alice, catalogers must run as fast as they can to remain in place."

IMAGINE HAVING at your fingertips a box of original reports from 1969 compiled by the crew of Apollo 12 as they conducted experiments on the surface of the moon. Imagine that these *Lunar Surface Experiments Package Status Reports,* which contain crucial research information, have been recently recovered and have not yet been made available to the planetary science community. Imagine the thrill of being responsible for scanning each document and making them available on the Web. Now stop imagining, because this is not fiction. This is one of David Bigwood's ongoing projects in his position at the Lunar and Planetary Institute (LPI) Library.

The Lunar and Planetary Institute, located in Houston, Texas, is a research institute that provides support services to NASA and the planetary science community. The institute's library, the Center for Information and Research Services, contains more than 50,000 cataloged monographs, slides, maps, and documents and more than 170 current journals and newsletters. The subject emphasis of the library's collection is primarily astronomy and geology. This collection is one of the eighteen international NASA Regional Planetary Image Facilities (RPIFs). "We have a mandate from NASA to provide access to mission imagery to the public," David says. "The RPIFs receive the images returned from planetary exploration missions and make them available to the public, whether it be an elementary schoolteacher, a textbook publisher, or the Discovery Channel."

Though his official title is assistant manager for library services, David's primary duty is cataloging. "About 60 percent of my time is spent cataloging," he says. "Much of our material is unique, so I do a lot of original cataloging. Most of our collection is in English, but we do have a good number of Russian items and some in other languages. The formats in the collection include texts, images, videos, globes, maps, electronic resources, models, and almost all formats other than music." When working on projects such as the Apollo-era collection, David scans documents and maps, adds metadata to the files, and makes them publicly accessible on the Web.

David also does some reference, web, and systems work. "Just as in other small libraries, most of us working here do many tasks," he says. "I am responsible for a weekly news page and podcast on our website. I participate in the SACO (Subject Authority Cooperative) Program and submit subject headings, cross-references, and classification numbers to the Library of Congress. As a cutting-edge research center, we are often among the first to publish and catalog new topics.

"Our primary patrons are the staff scientists and researchers doing related work at the Johnson Space Center," David says. "Working with them are the graduate assistants. We give them the same service as the staff scientists. Most of these users have their work routines and only require assistance occasionally. Those who need the most assistance are the student researchers in the summer intern program for upper-level undergraduates. They work one-on-one with staff scientists doing original research, and they are required to write an abstract and present their findings at the end of the summer. They are working within a short time frame and have the least experience using the materials. Many of these are the planetary scientists of tomorrow."

What David finds the most challenging about his job is the fact that cataloging is being completely overhauled thanks to technology. "Cataloging is in a state of flux at the moment," he says. "The basic manual catalogers use, the *Anglo-American Cataloging Rules*, is being redone as *Resource Description and Access*. The structure we have used since the late 1960s is being reconsidered. Rather than MARC (machine-readable cataloging) format, we may use some flavor of XML. The materials we are dealing with are coming in ever-increasing numbers of formats. Also, there is a growing interest outside of libraries in description and access. Archives, museums, computer scientists, and content producers are looking at markup and access issues."

David says that there is also a change in the tools used to store and display catalog records. The integrated library systems are splitting into distinct parts for staff and the public. "There is the addition of a social aspect to the public catalog," he explains. "The community can add comments, keywords or tags, bookmarks, display their latest reads, and share this with the wider community in some catalogs. This community involvement is something very new to our carefully constructed catalogs. How to best harness the wisdom of the crowd is yet to be decided."

Another challenge for David involves the increasing amount of material that is being licensed rather than owned. "The tools, structures, and work flows to deal with these items are still being developed," he says. "It is very possible for a library to purchase access to a journal from several different sources. Each of those sources will have a different license with different rules concerning interlibrary loan, off-site access, copying, reserve copies, etc. Each provider will index differently, provide different coverage, and have a different interface. A cataloger will find it difficult to make this clear through the catalog record."

David is very involved with social networks and experiments with social tools at work as well as for professional purposes outside of work. He writes a weekly column for the LPI called "What's New" that includes an RSS feed for flexible distribution. The column contains three to six short pieces of interest to the planetary science community and has information about holidays, special events at the LPI, trends, new additions to the collection, tips on using services, and information about scholarly publishing. "For a couple of years I did a podcast based on 'What's New,'" says David. "I read the online text with some concessions to spoken rather than written English. It was about five minutes long. I used open source software and a microphone. The only investment was the time involved to record, edit, and upload the file each week. At first we were getting over a hundred downloads per week. However, as time went by we noticed nobody ever mentioned listening to the podcast. We asked for feedback on the show and received none. After that, we announced we would stop the show unless anyone spoke up. Silence. It seems the show may have had plenty of downloads but few listens. We tried an experiment, but it was not something that connected with our users."

David recounts that he also tried to implement a MySpace page and a Facebook page for the library. Neither effort was successful at the time. "Our experiment may have been too early to have a positive result," he says. "More of the younger members of the planetary science community are now on Facebook. As they become a larger group, our presence there might become useful."

An example of social software that has connected well with the LPI community is Twitter. "We started using Twitter for connecting with our community," David says. "One year later, we have over 1,300 followers. They are a mix of people in the planetary science community, librarians, and local readers. We receive a couple of follower requests each day. The short messages we put on Twitter often get expanded treatment elsewhere, like in 'What's New.' Topics are pointers to resources and notices about the library, but might be more ephemeral or timely than the weekly treatment. For example, a stack of Apollo documents being put on the giveaway table would get mentioned here but nowhere else. This seems to have connected well with the community."

David is also responsible for the blog *Catalogablog* (http://catalogablog.blogspot .com), a site for news about cataloging and metadata. "When I started it in 2002, it was one of the first weblogs dealing with cataloging issues," he says. "I try to keep it professional, but it is mine and reflects my interests. I also use it as a place to experiment with a bit of metadata. Some posts include marked-up text, microformats, or metadata. I post about something I'll want to keep track of, want to read later, or want others to know about." The blog has increased David's visibility with groups of weblog authors and readers, and he will often be approached at conferences by people saying how the blog helped them at work or in graduate school. "Nice to know it's useful for someone other than myself," he says.

At the personal level, David has a MySpace page and a Facebook page, and he uses an RSS reader to keep track of some weblogs, such as *Planet Cataloging* (http://planetcataloging.org), as part of his professional reading. "Reading is required in many areas to stay current," he says. He also subscribes to several electronic discussion lists such as AUTOCAT (http://listserv.syr.edu/archives/autocat.html), an important source of communication among catalogers.

David first became interested in the library field through a young woman he was dating. "I was a few years out of college, having earned a B.A. in history from Assumption College in Worcester, Massachusetts. I was very dissatisfied with my career choice," he explains. "I was ready for a change. The woman I was seeing was a librarian and had been an archivist. As we dated I became familiar with the career and realized it was much more than stamping and shushing. It sounded like a very good match for me." He took a low-level reference position at the Houston Public Library and was happier there than he had been in years and decided this was the career for him. He earned his library science degree from the University of Texas at Austin and the University of North Texas. After graduating he was accepted for a technical services librarian position at the LPI. "I found I enjoyed tech services, especially cataloging, even more than reference," he says. "The nice thing about working at a small special library is that I get to do a bit of public service as well as cataloging; there are so few of us that everyone has to do a bit of everything."

David is a big believer in continuing education through professional memberships. He is a member of the Special Libraries Association, the Physics Astronomy Mathematics Division of SLA, the OLAC (Online Audiovisual Catalogers), and the Texas Library Association. In the past he was involved with Toastmasters International. "Public speaking is not something that came naturally to me," he says. "I had to work at it. Speaking before a group, whether it be a few coworkers at a staff meeting or a crowd full of colleagues at a natural conference, is all part of the profession. The skills I acquired at the local Toastmasters group have been invaluable.

"I think the ability to continue learning will be essential in the cataloging profession for the foreseeable future," David says. "There is just too much changing at the moment to rely on skills learned in graduate school. New technology, concepts, and tools will demand new skills. Like Alice, we must run as fast as we can to remain in place. If we want to make any progress we'll have to run even faster. I doubt cataloging in ten years will use many, if any, of the tools we now consider basic. For the next several years, change will be the only constant.

"One nice change is that technology has made communication much easier," David continues. "E-mail, chat, blogs, microblogging, and many other channels of exchanging and receiving information are all very useful. I get to one or two conferences a year. But with the new communication tools I am connected to the profession. No longer am I a lone cataloger or a lone planetary science librarian; now I have a connection to a wide community."

To library school students, David says, "Your education does not stop with the M.L.S. Your formal education might end there, but you must keep learning. Read books, articles, and online resources. Don't limit yourself to library science; many other fields can contribute to your success. Marketing, public relations, computer science, information architecture, and many other fields can all inform your work. Work on your writing, public speaking, budgeting, and networking skills. Take advantage of information education opportunities that become available.

"If you are interested in a career in cataloging, take some classes but also try to find an internship or volunteer at a local library doing cataloging," David concludes. "This not only will give you some practical experience but will also allow you to see if this is really what you want. If you are interested in special libraries, you need to educate yourself in the subject matter. A familiarity with the subject area is necessary, as is feeling comfortable with the topic. At an interview you have to be able to convince the interviewer that you are not afraid of the topic and are interested enough to stay current."

David recommends the following websites:

- http://units.sla.org/division/dpam/ (the Physics-Astronomy-Mathematics division of the Special Libraries Association)
- http://planetcataloging.org (Planet Cataloging—an aggregation of blogs related to cataloging and metadata)
- http://listserv.syr.edu/archives/autocat.html (AUTOCAT electronic discussion list for catalogers)
- http://olacinc.org/drupal/ (OLAC: Online Audiovisual Catalogers—the Internet and AV Media Catalogers Network)
- www.toastmasters.org (Toastmasters International: Become the Speaker and Leader You Want to Be)

ROSLYN DONALD

Business Librarian, San Mateo Public Library, San Mateo, California

"I attribute a lot of my success to being able to articulate the library's worth to businesspeople."

FEW PEOPLE think of public libraries as a place that can help with careers and business. Roslyn Donald is trying to change that, at least in the community of San Mateo, California. In her position, she makes every effort to convince the local business community that the library can save time and money in various ways. For her, promoting the library and its resources is an unwritten job responsibility.

As the business librarian at San Mateo Public Library, Roslyn spends about half of her time serving on the main reference desk answering both general and business questions. "Often, business folks will make an appointment with me if they want my undivided attention," she says. "I also get e-mail or phone referrals from other libraries or the city's business resource center. Sometimes I work on these requests while I'm on the desk; sometimes during off-desk time."

Roslyn's business clientele fall into three groups: job seekers, individual investors, and small business owners (either existing businesses or start-ups). "I would say that small business represents the largest number of reference requests," she says, "with job seekers being second and investors third. I think this has changed a lot in the last 8–10 years. The investor types used to be more prominent, but as financial information has moved to the Web, they have moved with it. Also, as brokerages start to offer more online services, these folks have less need of library services."

The library patrons who seek out Roslyn's help have a variety of backgrounds. "Most of my patrons have at least a four-year college education," she says, "and a large percentage have an advanced degree; San Mateo is a well-educated area. I see a lot of women changing careers, as well as computer/IT/financial types wanting to be self-employed as consultants. However, I'd say another 30 percent of my business patrons are recent immigrants who speak English as their second language, which can be especially challenging. Some are well educated in their home countries but very new to American life and customs. Others may not have graduated high school. These folks are more likely to be starting brick-and-mortar businesses such as landscaping, day care, restaurants, or import/export."

Roslyn has several additional responsibilities, including the maintenance of the library's home page and its calendar of events. She also represents the San Mateo

Public Library on the Information Services Committee of the Peninsula Library System Consortium. This committee is dedicated to refining the web catalog and making decisions about database subscriptions. She maintains the library's partnership with the San Francisco Small Business Development Center and manages a grant from the Certified Financial Planners' Board for financial planning workshops.

Roslyn is also involved with collection development. "I collect in several subject areas, including computers, personal finance, investing, folklore and social customs, careers, small businesses, and the trades," she says. "Plus, I often speak to community business groups to promote the library's business resources—business referral networks, job seeker support groups, Rotary and Kiwanis clubs, etc. The library recently became a cooperating collection of the Foundation Center, so I've been doing a lot of marketing to local nonprofits."

Roslyn says that being "technology literate" has helped her in her job. "Not only does it increase my productivity," she says, "it helps me stay in tune with concerns of the local, very technical business community (we're at the northern end of Silicon Valley)." She says that she has always been much more comfortable with technology than many of her peers. "My comfort level meant that I didn't spend much time wringing my hands about 'the way things used to be,'" she explains. "Now that I'm getting older, though, I can feel myself starting to get set in my ways, even as an avowed 'early adopter.' When new technology or tools come along, I purposely make myself try them. I want to *stay* comfortable with technology as it evolves. That's why I have a Facebook account and I at least tried Twitter before I gave up on it."

Roslyn is very proud of the "delicious" list (www.delicious.com/SanMateoLibrary/) she helped to create. "I attended a presentation about 'delicious' and other social bookmarking sites at Internet Librarian 2006 and was instantly captured by the possibilities," she says. Delicious (www.delicious.com) is a social bookmarking service that allows you to save all your bookmarks online, share them with other people, and see what other people are bookmarking. "The first thing I did when I got back was convert all our ready reference bookmarks to delicious, then I added everything that was on my personal desktop. It took a while to get the rest of the staff to use it, but now they are all fans."

Roslyn finds blogs to be useful in keeping up with changing technology and is a fan of *librarian.net* (www.librarian.net) and *Librarian in Black* (http://librarianinblack .net/librarianinblack/). "I have a home advantage," she says, "because my husband is a programmer, and he tells me about trends that he thinks might affect the library. We subscribe to *Wired, PC Magazine, MacTech,* and *Linux Journal* at home, to give you an idea of our dinner table conversation!" She attends conferences when the budget allows, and says that the Internet Librarian conference is an invaluable resource for learning about new technologies. She is also a member of the California Library Association.

Librarianship was not Roslyn's initial career choice. She has a B.S. in foreign service from the Georgetown University School of Foreign Service. "I often joke that my education prepared me well for working in the foreign land that is California!" she says. "The real reason the degree suited me is that I didn't have to pick a major, but could study all the history, political science, and languages that I wanted. My true need to be a generalist was showing." Right out of college, she worked as a clerk in a small law firm library. When she was sent to Lexis/Nexis training, she immediately "fell in love" with databases. After teaching English for a while in the People's Republic of China and Taiwan, she returned to the United States and decided to enroll in library school because she had loved using the databases in her first job.

While in the library school at San José State University, she worked for Information Access Company (now Cengage Gale) as an abstractor for Promt and as a project manager. The company offered tuition reimbursement. After graduating, she worked briefly at a couple of "dot-bombs" until the business librarian position became open at San Mateo Public Library. "I applied for the business librarian job as a joke," she says. "I had no real library experience, much less public library experience, and thought I didn't have a chance. However, I had a decent grasp of business jargon and structures due to my Promt abstracting experience, and I am strongly committed to the role of public libraries in our community. I guess they must have liked my jokes, because they hired me!"

In addition to being familiar with business jargon and basic business structures, Roslyn says that public speaking is a necessary skill for those interested in business librarianship. "I spend a lot of time and energy articulating the library's worth to businesspeople," she says. "Networking is also important, as is being technology literate. You have to truly enjoy helping people and talking to people about anything at all. If you prefer to spend your day just communing with your computer, look elsewhere. The librarian's role is not primarily research anymore; it's teaching and training and explaining the library's role in the community. Be sure that's what you want to do all day long before you commit to the M.L.S. degree.

"There is no pot of gold at the end of the rainbow! Don't expect to make much money," Roslyn advises. "You have to balance the day-to-day drudgery of 'Where's the bathroom?' and 'Why can't I get more time on the Internet?' with the more fulfilling aspects of the job. The days I spend enforcing policies and making grown-ups act like adults are the ones where I think, 'Just why did I get a master's degree?' But then there are the days when I talk to the patrons whose businesses take off with my help, or who have found great jobs, or just found a good book to read. Those are the days when I remember that this is the best job in the world."

NOTES

1. *Encyclopaedia Britannica*, "Eratosthenes of Cyrene," 2010, www.britannica.com/EBchecked/topic/191064/Eratosthenes-of-Cyrene.
2. Charles A. Crossley, "The Subject Specialist Librarian in an Academic Library: His Role and Place," *Aslib Proceedings* 26, no. 6 (1993): 236–49.
3. Lee Hadden, "Saint Lawrence: Patron of Librarians and Archivists," 1999, http://valinor.ca/lawrence.html.
4. Special Libraries Association, "About Information Professionals," 2009, www.sla.org/content/SLA/professional/index.cfm.
5. Ohio University Libraries, "The Subject Librarian: Role and Responsibilities," 2009, www.library.ohiou.edu/info/colldev/librarians.html.
6. Stephen Pinfield, "The Changing Role of Subject Librarians in Academic Libraries," *Journal of Librarianship and Information Science* 33, no. 1 (March 2001): 32–38.

CHAPTER 2

LIBRARIANS AS TECHNOLOGY GURUS AND SOCIAL NETWORKERS

LIBRARY 2.0, virtual reference, Second Life Library, mobile technology, Next Generation librarianship, the Semantic Web, wireless technology, metadata, e-publishing,
mashups, social networking, Twitter, Facebook. It's hard to believe that a mere ten
years ago, any (or all) of these terms might have resulted in frowns of confusion on
the faces of librarians. Now these phrases are tossed about in frequent professional
conversation and have, in fact, been the cause of much upheaval in librarianship.

Let's face it. Because of technology, the libraries of today seem to bear little
resemblance to the warehouses of knowledge that characterized libraries of the past.
Physical walls and endless shelves are no longer requirements for libraries as more and
more resources become "virtual." Electronic journals, books, and databases provide
instant access to information, and library patrons can remain in the comfort of their
own homes or offices to make use of library materials. This upheaval may seem a
threat to librarianship, but in fact the opposite is true. When librarians keep up with
technology, adapt to change, and match library services to current technological trends,
they reinforce the fact that librarians are more invaluable than ever.

Though the "physical space" of the library has changed, the role of the librarian has
not changed. The role of the librarian, even in this "Web 2.0 world," is still the same
as it has always been: to connect people with information. For centuries, librarians
have served to help connect fields of knowledge. The twenty-first-century librarian
simply does this increasingly in a virtual space, as opposed to a physical one. The

mission of librarians has always been threefold: to create conversations, to encourage connections, and to build community. Technology simply offers methods of fulfilling that mission in new and interesting ways.

Librarians who are experts in technology—technology gurus—are fast becoming sought-after commodities in the library world. These are the librarians who deliberately immerse themselves in technology, who embrace change without fear; who, in fact, position themselves as agents of change, and who use technology to place library services exactly where they are needed within their communities. Library administrators realize that these are the kinds of people who can solidly launch libraries into the Web 2.0 environment and ensure the future of librarianship. If you have a "knack" for technology; if you have a solid background in all things technology-related; if you learn quickly and are not afraid of change; and if you are willing to "stick your neck out" to try new things, you are in a very fortunate position. With a little on-the-job experience under your belt, you will be able to shape your career into anything you want it to be.

SOCIAL NETWORKING

The original intention was for "technology gurus" and "social networkers" to have separate chapters in this book. It soon became apparent, however, that the line between the two groups is markedly fuzzy. Those with expertise in technology tend to be excellent with social software. Not only do they understand how the technology works, but they have no fear of experimenting with the various social software options to see what works and what doesn't in different library environments. The technology gurus of the library world, then, are often the social networking experts as well.

Librarians as social networkers have the unique role of using Web 2.0 communication tools to link people to information and to promote library services. Some of the tools commonly used are blogs, wikis, RSS feeds, podcasts, instant messaging, Flickr, vodcasts, and mashups.[1] Twenty-first-century librarians must understand not only how to use and market these tools but also know how to help patrons use them effectively. They have to be able to compare different versions of software to determine which will best meet patron needs. No matter what the library environment, the time is right for more librarians to explore how these social tools can enhance communication with users. Academic librarians can use social tools to reach out to faculty and students. Public librarians can use social tools to reach out to patrons where they are "living" on the Web. School librarians can use social tools to create spaces for collaboration and learning. Entrepreneurial librarians can use social software to find new ways of delivering information to clients and staff.[2] Should the library have a Facebook page? Will Twitter help reach out to younger audiences? Should the library have a virtual reference desk? Would having an avatar in Second Life help promote library services? These are the types of questions that librarians involved with social networking are charged with answering. How fun is this?

For librarians, "the sky is the limit" when it comes to using social networking tools to connect to library users. Michael Stephens, librarian, author, and technology trainer (featured later in this book), says it best: "Let us, as librarians, the navigators of the Information Age, help grow communities, all kinds of communities, professional and personal—from librarians who create trading cards, to folks who like Macs, to people who love their dogs—and let's meet up and swap stories, both online and in person! Come in, the water is fine."[3]

ENVIRONMENTS

Any type of library—whether physical or virtual, academic or public—has a need for librarians specializing in technology or social software. Some technology gurus featured in the upcoming spotlights work for public libraries and some for academic libraries, while others work independently. The social networkers work in both academic and public libraries as well. Some of the featured librarians are known as technology gurus or social networkers outside of their "day jobs." Librarians with these skills are not limited to any particular environment because, simply put, there are no walls or boundaries for technology.

RESPONSIBILITIES

Specific job duties will vary depending on the exact nature of the position, the client or patron base, and the institutional climate. Below are some common responsibilities for librarians involved with technology and social networking.

Explore and advocate emerging technologies. The emergence of new software, hardware, devices, and tools is constant. This is perhaps the most time-consuming responsibility. It is difficult to keep up with emerging technologies and labor-intensive to test them. This is where it becomes important to build a strong network of colleagues with whom to share ideas and learn from other experts. Most technology gurus know that they cannot be successful if they are "alone."

Provide training associated with the introduction of new technologies. Once a new tool or product has been tested and deemed acceptable for the particular environment, the technology librarian is usually responsible for training staff and library patrons to use it effectively.

Maintain networks, computers, and servers. These tasks are vital in both traditional and virtual libraries. This is never more clear than when there is a power failure. The next time there is a power failure when you are in a library, take note of the mad scramble that ensues. Without functional computers and software, most modern libraries are like fish out of water. The librarians providing technical support are invaluable. System upgrades, new installation, backups, and enhancements all fall within this area of responsibility.

Website development and maintenance. Technology gurus are generally web-savvy and find this particular responsibility to be a natural extension of their interests. Creating and maintaining blogs, wikis, Facebook pages, and so on are common tasks that fall within this category.

Support online learning and instructional services. In academic institutions, technology librarians are often involved with the provision of technical support for online learning or distance education.

Committee and liaison work. Unless working as an entrepreneur or a solo librarian, most technology gurus or social networkers are involved in committee work or serve as liaisons between the library and internal or external communities.

SKILLS

It is a given that librarians involved with technology should be proficient in such things as word processing, web navigation and design, network and file management, and so on. The list would be too long to include here. Equally as important as the specific technical skills are the "big picture" skills that will help librarians keep up with technology, make good decisions about implementing new technologies, and advocate for those technologies.[4] Below is a list of these "big picture" skills.

- ability to embrace change
- ability to test and evaluate new technologies
- ability to assess the technology needs of library patrons and staff
- ability to learn new technologies with ease
- ability to teach new technologies to others
- ability to keep up with new trends in technology and librarianship

- project management skills
- ability to sell ideas/market technology to administrators

The following is a list of technology trends that librarians as technology gurus or social networkers should be conversant with:[5]

- social software
- open source software
- mobile information devices
- collaboration tools
- Second Life
- cloud architecture
- wireless technology
- mashups
- streaming media
- catalog overlays

EDUCATION AND TRAINING

Most positions require a master's degree in library and information science from an ALA-accredited institution. Specialized training, such as an undergraduate degree in computer science, is not required, but is generally preferred. Many librarians who are self-professed technology gurus have acquired their skills in a variety of ways, including formal training, continuing education, reading professional literature, interaction with professional colleagues, and trial and error.

PROFESSIONAL ASSOCIATIONS

Below is a list of associations recommended by the various librarians "spotlighted" in this chapter:

- American Library Association (ALA)—www.ala.org
  - *Library and Information Technology Association (LITA)*
    www.lita.org
  - *Association of College and Research Libraries (ACRL)*
    www.acrl.org

- *Reference and User Services Association (RUSA)*
  www.ala.org/rusa/
- *Public Library Association (PLA)*
  www.pla.org/

■ ASIS&T (American Society for Information Science and Technology)—
www.asis.org

■ Regional and local library associations

SPOTLIGHTS

MICHAEL SAUERS

Technology Innovation Librarian, Nebraska Library Commission, Lincoln, Nebraska

"I love to figure out technology and then explain it to end-users."

MICHAEL SAUERS calls himself a librarian, trainer, and writer. When examining a snapshot of his professional activities, it's hard to say which role takes top priority. He is the author of ten books related to technology and libraries, including his most recent book entitled *Blogging and RSS: A Librarian's Guide* (2nd ed.). He has written numerous articles for various journals and magazines; he gives multiple presentations each year at conferences; he is the author of blogs and contributor to podcasts; he runs websites for authors and historical societies; and he is an avid photographer and reader of books. Oh yes, he also has a full-time job!

In his position as the technology innovation librarian for the Nebraska Library Commission, Michael's responsibilities include keeping up with the latest trends and technologies, evaluating them for use in a library environment, and passing what he's learned along to other librarians. The Nebraska Library Commission is a statewide organization whose mission is the promotion, development, and coordination of library and information services. Michael spends much of his time teaching workshops for librarians within the state of Nebraska. These training sessions are designed to support Nebraska libraries in their cooperative efforts to share resources and services. Workshop topics focus on the electronic exchange of information and can be about reference services, web design, or the use of information technologies.

Michael's primary clientele are all of the librarians and library staff in Nebraska. The level of knowledge and comfort with technology varies widely among these groups. "I get most excited when I can see the lightbulb turn on over someone's head in a class," he says. "Better yet is when, during a class, someone asks a question that is directly related to what I was going to cover next. I get goose bumps whenever this happens. Not only does this show that they've understood the material so far, but also that they are able to anticipate what's next without even realizing it. When this happens, I know I'm doing it right.

"The most challenging part is when you've tried explaining something six ways to Sunday and someone just isn't getting it," he continues. "Over the past fifteen years I've learned to have a lot of patience. Sometimes, though, it's difficult not to just say, 'Here, let me do it.' If you do it for them, they never learn it." Patience is a necessary skill for Michael's line of work.

When he is not teaching, preparing for a workshop, or attending committee meetings, Michael spends his time researching new technologies. "Technology *is* my job," he says. "You'll typically find me doing anything from reading blogs and feeds to reading professional journals or books. I regularly have three computers (two desktops and a laptop) hooked up and running on my desk." He also works directly with libraries to assist them with technology questions and problems. In 2008 he planned and implemented a statewide WiFi technology grant funded by the Gates Foundation. This project enabled fifty libraries to each receive a basic WiFi router and state-of-the-art laptop in order to be able to offer WiFi to library users.

"What is most unique about my job," Michael says, "is the fact that I'm pretty much left in control of what I do, how I do it, and when I do it. Granted, there are meetings that are scheduled, conferences to attend, and specific projects that my boss wants me to do, but in the end I'm generally in control."

Michael says that he became interested in librarianship "for the most clichéd of reasons." Namely, his love of books. His undergraduate degree is a B.S. in American studies from SUNY at Brockport. "By the end of my undergraduate career, I'd worked in bookstores for almost a decade and thought that libraries would be a great career," he says. He earned his master of library science degree from SUNY at Albany.

"Getting into the technology end of librarianship was completely unplanned," he says. His first computer was an Atari 400 that he received when he was thirteen years old. When he entered Albany's M.L.S. program he quickly discovered the Internet (the early days of Gopher, Telnet, and FTP) and became "hooked." Since there were few technology courses offered in library school at the time, Michael found and took courses in database management and programming from other departments. Beyond that, he says, "when it comes to technology, I'm pretty much completely self-taught."

The Internet 101 course he took in library school was the catalyst for his role as technology instructor. Toward the end of the semester, Michael mentioned to the instructor that there was this "new thing" called "the Web" and a "browser" called Lynx and that it was going to replace Gopher. He was graciously told to sit down. At the next class session, Michael tried again. "I told him of this new 'HTML language' and that creating web pages was much easier than creating Gopher sites and that I'd already taught myself how." Again, he was politely told to have a seat. Finally, during the last class of the semester, the instructor told the class that they may have heard about this new "web thing" in the Internet but that he hadn't had a chance to look at it. "However," said the instructor, "Michael knows all about it, so let's have him come up and tell us about it." Michael ended up teaching that portion of the class for the next three semesters and hasn't stopped since.

Michael says that his methodology for keeping up with technology is threefold. "First, I read everything I can get my hands on." Between blogs, feeds, magazines, journals, and the occasional newspaper, he is constantly on the lookout for updates and new technologies. "Second, I utilize video and audio podcasts. Third, and probably most importantly, I play with technology as much as I can. If I read about a new piece of hardware, I try to get my hands on it. If I hear about a new social network, I sign up. I've got so many accounts I've forgotten most of them. The point is to get on, play, and see what sticks."

Michael is often invited to be a guest speaker at professional conferences. "I like to joke that I don't really *attend* conferences anymore since I'm generally presenting at them," he says. "I do stick around to hear as many of the other speakers as I can, though." He is committed to attending Computers in Libraries as well as Internet Librarian each year. On the state level, he attends the annual Nebraska Library Association (NLA) conference, of which he is a member. He currently serves as the vice-chair/chair-elect of the NLA's Information Technology and Access Round Table.

While technology encompasses every aspect of his professional activities, Michael does not insist that every librarian needs to be a technology guru in order to survive. "But," he says, "all librarians do need to have a certain minimal level of comfort with technology. Being a technophobe or just being afraid to try new things will only make your job harder and make your patrons appreciate the library less in the long run."

Michael says that for those interested in a job similar to his, there are two must-have skills. The first is the ability to constantly learn. "The concept of lifelong learning might be a cliché to some," he says, "but in a position like mine, if you're not willing to constantly learn, you just can't do this job." The second skill is the ability to effectively pass knowledge along to others. He says that knowing how to do something and having the ability to teach someone else how to do it are two completely different things. "Think about it," he says. "How many IT people have you met that are 100 percent certain they know what they are doing but when you ask them to explain it to you, you're lost about ten words in? Having the ability to teach others enables you to be successful at a job like mine."

To Michael, the meaning of librarianship is still the same as always: assisting others in fulfilling their information needs. "What has changed in the past decade is the role of technology in doing that," he says. "Some librarians think that the increasing role of technology in the profession has changed the profession itself. I honestly don't agree with that point of view." Much has changed since he entered the profession in 1995. To him, though, the most significant change has been the rise of the Internet. At the start of his career, few libraries offered Internet access. "Now, a library without the Internet is considered the exception."

Michael's advice to new librarians is this: "Be willing to constantly learn. Be willing to try new things. Have a good bedside/deskside manner when it comes to helping people with technology."

Michael recommends the following websites:

- www.travelinlibrarian.info (his own site, The Travelin' Librarian)
- www.nlc.state.ne.us (the Nebraska Library Commission)
- www.nebraskalibraries.org/ITART/ (NLA's Information Technology and Access Round Table)
- http://tisfortraining.wordpress.com (T is for Training)
- http://revision3.com (Revision3: Internet Television)
- www.twit.tv (TWiT.TV)

JESSAMYN WEST

Community Technologist, Randolph, Vermont

"Technology is indivisible from the work that I do."

Jessamyn West is a free spirit when it comes to work. The traditional 9-to-5 "day job" not being quite her cup of tea, she divides her time among various professional responsibilities that fall under the purview of community technology. "I have about five different jobs ranging from being an in-person librarian at a rural library to being a community moderator on a massive group blog," she says.

Once a week, Jessamyn dons her "technology instructor" hat and runs a Q&A drop-in at the local vocational high school. "I literally hang out in a computer lab in the afternoon and wait for people to come by with technology questions," she explains. Between three and seven people per week take advantage of the technology drop-in. Often these are retirees in their seventies or eighties who have computer questions or who want to learn to use the Internet in order to stay in touch with family members or shop online. Sometimes she helps tradespeople who need to learn technology to keep up at work, people needing typing practice, or folks who don't know how to look up a URL or search the Internet. "Often they are well-educated people who feel stupid because they're not tech-savvy, and I think that's a shame."

In the evenings, Jessamyn teaches basic computer skills classes such as Getting Started with Excel or Photoshop Elements. In addition, she works part-time for the Tunbridge Public Library, where she is responsible for maintaining the public and staff computers and automating the library. She takes pride in being both very good with technology and able to explain the technology to a novice. She feels that this unusual combination of skills, along with living in a rural area, makes her particular skill set "pretty desirable."

The human relations component of these jobs is particularly exciting to Jessamyn. "I meet people I would never cross paths with if I just hung around online all the time," she says. "Since one of my other side jobs is lifeguarding at the local pool, I often see my students swimming, or at the store or movie theater. Being a part of a small-town community means you don't just teach when you're on the job. Once people know you're good with computers, you get buttonholed at parties and asked about this or that technology topic. I sort of like it; I wouldn't be involved in this sort of thing if I didn't."

Another of her job titles is online community moderator for MetaFilter.com. *MetaFilter* is a community weblog to which anyone can contribute. Currently there

are over 40,000 members of this massive group blog. Jessamyn is respo
maintaining ask.metafilter.com, a community question-and-answer resource. She
maintains the FAQ, answers member questions, creates and enforces site guidelines,
and helps maintain the off-site wiki. "*MetaFilter* is basically a social network, a huge
one that I've had a part in creating," she says. "I do this job when I want, and where
I want, and all I need is access to the Internet. I have no schedule, office, or even job
description." Her position with *MetaFilter* is a unique arrangement between her and
the owner of the site, and she professes to take home a decent salary. "It's sort of the
telecommuting job of the future that we all hoped the Internet might bring but only
did in really rare cases."

In her remaining free time, Jessamyn is a columnist for *Computers in Libraries.*
Her bimonthly column called "Tech Tips" outlines simple technological advice and
strategies for small and tech-poor libraries. In addition, she is often invited to give
talks and workshops on technology and library topics to various organizations. Finally,
she writes articles and book chapters on topics ranging from open source software
to web design.

When asked for the source of Jessamyn's affinity for technology, she replies, "I
grew up in a techie household. My dad worked in computers back in the 1970s and
'80s (you can read about him in Tracy Kidder's book *Soul of a New Machine*), and so
I grew up knowing the lingo before I even knew much about computers."

After graduating from Hampshire College with a B.A. in linguistics, Jessamyn
had to determine the educational direction she wanted to take next. She had been
working a temp job in Seattle after moving there from New England, and thought
she might want to go to law school. After taking the LSATs and getting accepted to
a law school, she had second thoughts. "I realized that I was considering going into
debt for a profession that was going to require me to dress up and fight with people
a lot. Neither appealed to me." She recalled that as an undergraduate, she enjoyed
researching papers much more than actually writing them. "The University of Washington was right up the street," she says, "and had cheap tuition for in-staters as
well as a decent library school, so I decided to go there." Her M.L.I.S. studies at the
University of Washington Information School focused on Internet instruction and
bibliographic instruction.

"As far as technology goes, being at the University of Washington was the real
catalyst for me because they had an amazing Computer Science Department that
worked closely with the library," she says. "There was a lot of technology available
to play with, along with a robust support structure. The OPAC they were using while
I was in library school—Willow, an X-Windows graphical user interface that was
almost completely customizable—remains to this day the best OPAC I've ever used."

Jessamyn says that the best class she took in library school was a class called Service to Special Populations. "I learned a lot about usability and how it relates to libraries, and how users with special needs deserve the same access to public services as everyone else," she explains. "I spend a lot of time thinking about those sorts of things when I design websites or any new technology tool for small public libraries." Her work for small public libraries is rewarding, partly because there isn't usually a lot of red tape or resistance to new technology initiatives. "If you're willing to do the work, and I am," she says, "there is not much resistance to technology because people realize that technology solves problems and doesn't create them." She says that serious technology implementation needs to involve everyone on a library staff, and not be handed down from top administration without first getting everyone to buy into the idea. "I'm very sympathetic to technostress, but I'm not satisfied with 'no' as an answer."

To keep up with technology, Jessamyn finds herself going outside of traditional library-oriented professional development opportunities. For example, she recently attended the SXSW (South by Southwest) Interactive conference and "met a lot of people who are doing really cutting-edge things with technology." (SXSW is an organization joining key players in the interactive, film, video game, and music industries.) "It was great to spend a set of days with people for whom technology is a given in their lives," she says, "not something to be fought with and argued against."

At library-related conferences, Jessamyn is usually the person teaching courses rather than attending them. She speaks and teaches at 10–15 conferences per year. "I learn a lot by teaching other people," she says. "Also, I got a lot of my skills outside of librarianship. I can bring those to the profession as a sort of 'outsider' while still understanding the values and restrictions of library work." She is a member of the Vermont Library Association and serves as its webmaster.

Jessamyn's unique approach to librarianship is not for everyone. "People e-mail me a lot saying 'I'd like to have jobs like yours,' and the first thing I do is try to dissuade them," she says. "Not because I don't love what I do but because my job often lacks what many people want in a career: money, stability, and regularity." It was only recently, after over thirteen years in the profession, that she started making what she considers a decent and regular salary. "I've never put financial matters at the top of my list, but that's mainly because I have been privileged enough to have gotten through college and grad school without assuming any debt, and also because I'm comfortable with a pretty-low-on-the-food-chain existence. I don't have kids or even a cat to support, so it's easy for me to live this way. I prefer it, actually, but it's not for everyone. Mainly, I like to say that it's okay to create your own life and job, but you're unlikely to be able to do it within the confines of a traditional library job.

"I think that when most people think 'technology gurus,' they don't think 'librarians,'" concludes Jessamyn. "I'm happy to help change their minds."

If you'd like to learn more about Jessamyn and her professional activities, visit her blog at librarian.net (www.librarian.net) or her personal blog (www.jessamyn.com/journal/). She recommends the following:

- http://the23thingsproject.pbworks.com (the 23 Things Web 2.0 Project, designed to help librarians and educators learn key technology skills)
- www.libsuccess.org (Library Success: A Best Practices Wiki)

MICHELE LIPSON

Computer Services Librarian, Bryant Library, Roslyn, New York

"The most important skills for a librarian specializing in technology or computer services are flexibility and the appreciation of change. Curiosity and tenacity are also key."

MICHELE LIPSON is the computer services librarian at Bryant Library, the oldest continuing public library in Nassau County, New York. Her work involves two distinct sets of clientele: the public (a population of over 18,000 educated and well-read people) and the librarians at Bryant Library. "I split my time between educating our patrons as well as training our librarians," she says.

Michele's responsibilities are numerous. She maintains a suite of electronic databases, which involves troubleshooting and repair and the collection of usage statistics. She is also involved with the evaluation and selection of databases for the various library departments, and she assists the Public Relations Department in the promotion of databases through the design of fliers, bookmarks, and brochures. She manages the library's website and collaborates with departments regarding website content. She develops technology-based programs that are offered to the public, writes a bimonthly "NewsBytes" column for the newsletter, and writes the library's blog. "Our blog was the first public library blog in the county and has been used as a teaching model," she says.

Michele is also responsible for the design and maintenance of the library's wikis. There is a public wiki containing recommended websites, and there is an internal reference wiki through which librarians share information. She oversees the computer volunteers who assist patrons with computer use, keeps statistics on web page hits and the use of the public computers, and works with the computer technician to ensure that all computers, printers, scanners, and other equipment remain in good working order. Finally, she takes daily shifts at the reference desk, helps the Circulation Department to oversee the online ordering of interlibrary loan materials, attends workshops, and reads technology- and library-related blogs and journal articles.

Michele's day-to-day routine varies, but in general she begins and ends her day online. She reads e-mail first thing in the morning, flagging those that need to be dealt with soon and sorting others that can wait. Next, she checks to see what materials have arrived through the interlibrary loan system, what is still on order and what might be overdue. After handling any computer issues that have cropped up since the night before, she begins to tackle her never-ending list of tasks. "There may be a web link that is broken, an image that needs replacing, or a database that is giving us a problem," she explains. "I run statistics once a month—this takes several painstaking days at the beginning of every month. I write a blog entry once or twice per week, publicizing a library event, a new book, or a library-related item. I also tend to the internal reference wiki every day, either removing old entries or entering new ones.

"The most exciting part of my job is learning something new every day," says Michele. Being deeply involved with technology requires constant learning, and she makes every effort to keep up. "This is not the kind of job where you can relax once you obtain your degree," she explains. "No, this is an exciting time to be a librarian, and change is constant." She reads professional journals, newspapers, and keeps up with many blogs. She attends webinars (web-based seminars) and continuing education workshops. She is a member of the Nassau County Library Association and attends that conference annually, and she follows national conferences online. "Continuing education is ongoing and important," she says. "All of my technological experience was self-motivated and either self-taught or sought out." She feels fortunate that her employer is supportive of continuing education.

"Librarians in other departments keep up with their particular niches," says Michele, "but they depend on me to bring new technology, databases, and programs to their attention." For example, she teaches an online summer class that the reference librarians are required to complete. The course lasts 6–8 weeks and includes instruction in databases that are new, underutilized, or have changed during the past year. Michele also includes technology education that she feels is necessary in our profession. For instance, this past summer she included a component on using YouTube as a search engine and a reference source, as well as a section on instant messaging.

Social networking is important to Michele both personally and professionally. She joined Facebook while in an earlier position working as a young adults librarian because she felt it was a necessary part of the job. "Now that I am in a different position, I find it even more important," she says. "Not only my friends and family but also our patrons and colleagues are online now. I also have a LibraryThing and Shelfari page, I have a screen name, and I keep up with the library blog and wikis." During the day, she often uses Google Chat and Trillian to quickly and easily communicate with colleagues. She rarely has time to check Facebook during working hours, so she uses her free time in the evenings to log on and keep up with friends and colleagues.

"Technology has radically altered the path of my career," Michele says. "I began working with children and then young adults when I saw how the rise of technology was taking off. I caught that wave and ran with it as my own children struggled to keep up. Databases and the Web are more than tools for librarians to use. It is so exciting to be part of this generation of rapid changes. It is that excitement that has kept me going. I love finding new ways of incorporating technology into our jobs."

Michele says that technology has changed librarianship throughout the course of her career. "Librarians used to be the experts in the field of finding answers to questions," she says. "Now, many people believe themselves to be searchers. But, as we know, a basic Google search is not the only way to find answers. You have to know how to do an advanced search, how to evaluate web pages, and how to decide if what you're looking for is better sought in a database." She says that a librarian's job has changed to incorporate answering technology-related questions such as "How do I download an audiobook to my iPod?" or "How can I crop this photo?" or "How can I scan my résumé?" Librarians now must be technologically prepared. "Patrons don't always realize that technology has made librarians even more essential," Michele continues. "They may not need us to find out the names of the Seven Dwarfs, but they still need us to field the more complicated reference questions."

Michele received her bachelor of arts degree from Hampshire College in Amherst, Massachusetts. To complete the program, she wrote a 100-page thesis that explored the effectiveness of bibliotherapy on children of divorced parents. This project allowed her to explore the children's rooms of many Massachusetts libraries. When she graduated, she continued to feel a pull toward libraries, so she took a job at a local library doing programming for fifth and sixth graders. The position did not require an M.L.S. "I found myself surrounded by nurturing and supportive children's librarians who encouraged me to get my library degree," she says. The following year, a young adult librarian vacancy became available, and Michele was offered the position if she would agree to enroll in an M.L.S. program. She agreed, and received her master of library science degree from St. John's University.

Michele's "advice from a 'techie' librarian" is this: "Go for it! Read, read, read about technology and how it relates to libraries. Experiment, play, have fun, be creative, don't be afraid to fail, talk to other professionals and listen. Our role is changing so rapidly that we are in the fortunate position of creating our own jobs. We are no longer just selecting books—we are technology specialists, web designers, blog authors, web searchers, and information professionals. If you put yourself out there, online, you can potentially have a following and interact with patrons and professionals from all over the world!

"I believe that there will always be a role for librarians in our society," she concludes. "However, we need to promote ourselves and our skills and continue to offer what patrons need. In order to keep ourselves relevant, we must be one step ahead of our patrons. For example, since we know that teens are communicating mainly through text messaging these days, libraries should consider offering reference help via text. If adult patrons are on Facebook, libraries should ensure that library events are listed on Facebook and should try to engage these groups in library-related conversation. We should offer online research assistance 24/7. The point is to keep up with our patrons or we will lose them as readers, participants, and budget-passing taxpayers."

To learn more about Michele and her projects, visit the Bryant Library blog at www.nassaulibrary.org/bryant/blog/.

GREG SCHWARTZ

Library Systems Manager, Louisville Free Public Library, Louisville, Kentucky

"Technology, of course, is my job."

It is Greg Schwartz's job to make sure that over 850 workstations and thirty servers work properly on a daily basis. This seemingly daunting responsibility falls on his shoulders because he is the systems manager of a seventeen-branch county library system in Louisville, Kentucky.

Greg's position at the Louisville Free Public Library consists of two central components. The majority of his time is consumed with management of the day-to-day IT operations. Luckily, however, he does not work alone. "I have five very knowledgeable employees who make all the magic happen," he says. "My ability to handle tech problems has grown by leaps and bounds and I learn more every single day," he says, "but it's not really why I'm here. I manage. I make decisions. I order things. I sign time sheets. I handle crises. I do what I can to help and, oftentimes, that has less to do with technology and more to do with customer service and communication skills."

The second component of his job involves participation on a four-person innovation team. The team consists of the library systems manager (himself), the manager of computer services (Greg's boss), a systems engineer (whom he refers to as "the IT genius"), and the digital services manager (the web designer).

"There is no routine day," Greg says. "This is one of the best things about the position." He starts off every morning by running through a routine to make sure all services are functioning properly and that they are ready for the public. The rest of his day is never set in stone, and he finds this exciting. "I interact primarily with the organization's staff," he says. "But we are all working to serve the public—in particular, the people of Jefferson County, Kentucky. With the high number of people in our service area, we encounter all demographics."

Greg's background, before becoming a librarian, was in food service. Despite his bachelor's degree in the history of art in architecture, he found himself in a series of management positions in various restaurants and kitchens. He moved around a bit after graduation and then met his future wife in Boulder, Colorado. When she went to law school in Eugene, Oregon, he followed her there and began visiting the Eugene Public Library. "I noticed the reference librarian scurrying around helping people," he recounts. "It looked tailor-made for a person who loved looking things up, but not writing them down. And, of course, I needed to find something a little more profitable and reliable than kitchen work. That's how I ended up at UIUC (University of Illinois at Urbana-Champaign), where I received my M.S.L.I.S."

Greg says that he had always been drawn to technology, but primarily as an end-user or consumer. "I was exposed young," he claims. "I had a Commodore 64 in my bedroom when I was eight. I'm not a coder or someone who really has genuine interest in the under-the-hood aspects of computing. I'm interested in what technology does for me and, in turn, other people."

He knows how important it is to keep up with technology, particularly in his position as systems manager. "There are constantly new challenges emerging and ways to improve the services we already provide," he says. "It requires me to stay current and think innovatively at all times." Consequently, he uses RSS as his primary tool for keeping current. He follows over 200 RSS feeds covering a variety of topics in librarianship and technology. "I do attend professional conferences, but primarily as a speaker and networker. My 'keeping current' strategies tend to put me out in front of most of the relevant conference content. But the experiences are immensely valuable, even if the content of the sessions doesn't always transform your worldview." Greg is a "proud member" of the Library Society of the World (http://thelsw.org).

Greg has been involved in a number of what he calls "extracurricular projects" involving social networking. One of these was the *Carnival of the Infosciences* (http://infosciences.pbworks.com), a biweekly weblog post "that endeavors to showcase the best posts in the blogosphere about topics related to the wide world of Library and Information Science." He created the weblog in 2005 and then passed the administration over to someone else. "My extremely limited notoriety in librarianship is more likely a result of my adventures in podcasting, starting with the podcast that shared a name and web space with my blog, *Open Stacks* (http://openstacks.net/os/)." More recently, Greg has been the host of Uncontrolled Vocabulary (http://uncontrolledvocabulary.com), a weekly round table discussion of "all things library and librarianship."

Greg says that these social networking activities don't tie directly into his "day job," but they certainly make him better equipped to succeed at his job. "They force me to keep current and to know what's going on around me," he says. Other skills that are helpful to Greg in both his day job and his social networking are good communication skills, patience, and tireless dedication to self-education.

To those asking for advice in a career similar to his, Greg responds, "Get ready for a dogfight. There are lots of talented people joining the profession who are mobile and more willing to relocate than ever." He says that librarians should definitely be proficient in technology, but they also need to develop and maintain their proficiencies in many arenas.

"It takes a wide range of skills to be effective in this field," Greg concludes. "Librarians need to experiment with the ever-increasing number of tools available to them to increase their skills, strengthen their collegial networks, and ultimately provide better service to their patrons."

To learn more about Greg, you can follow him on Twitter or FriendFeed under the user name gregschwartz. He also recommends joining the IEEE Computer Society (www.computer.org) for access to a wide range of low-cost, online IT training.

MEREDITH FARKAS

Head of Instructional Initiatives, Kreitzberg Library, Norwich University, Northfield, Vermont

"I am a librarian, a writer, a teacher, and a tech geek."

As THE head of instructional initiatives at the Kreitzberg Library at Norwich University, Meredith Farkas is responsible for coordinating information literacy instruction. This involves improving the way librarians teach, marketing library instruction to faculty and administrators, developing assessment tools, and keeping track of statistics. She does a lot of teaching and is the academic liaison to the social sciences. She also shares the responsibilities of providing reference assistance and serving on various committees.

"The thing I like most about my job is that there's never a typical day," Meredith says. "Some days I do a lot of teaching, other days I'm weeding or ordering books for the collection, other days I'm building web tutorials. Because we are a small library, I get to be involved in many different aspects of the library's operation—everything from covering the circulation desk to working on next year's budget. It's challenging because there's never enough time to do everything we'd like to accomplish, but it's also great because our work is never done. I'm the sort of person who becomes easily bored with things and I never get bored in my current position."

Kreitzberg Library's primary clientele are students and faculty. On-campus students are comprised mostly of undergraduates, while the distance learners (about half of the student body) are graduate students. Many of the university's faculty are actively involved in research, which Meredith and her colleagues help to facilitate with collections and research assistance. Meredith's secondary clientele are the other librarians who provide instruction and to whom she is charged with providing training.

Meredith utilizes software related to the creation of course guides and tutorials, such as wikis, screencasting software, and web authoring software. She administers the library's server and maintains the library's blogs, wikis, and IM (instant message) reference service. "I do a lot of things that are probably not traditionally the job of an instruction librarian, but they are a consequence of my being tech-savvy and eager to improve our services," says the self-proclaimed "tech geek." Meredith's knowledge of technology in libraries has landed her a columnist position with *American Libraries* magazine. She writes the column called "Technology in Practice" that focuses on successful uses of technology by libraries.

Meredith is passionate about incorporating social software into library services. In the spring of 2007, her book *Social Software in Libraries: Building Collaboration,*

Communication, and Community Online was published by Information Today. The work is a "nuts-and-bolts book" that introduces social technologies and demonstrates how they're being implemented in libraries today. Continuing the social software theme, she and five other librarians developed a free online course for librarians called "Five Weeks to a Social Library." The course provided a "social online learning opportunity" for librarians to learn about social software and how to use it in their libraries. Since the program was a great success, Meredith hopes that other libraries and organizations will replicate the course model.

Known by some as the "Queen of Wikis," Meredith is the creator of "Library Success: A Best Practices Wiki" (www.libsuccess.org), which collects best practices and useful resources from others in the profession. She has created several other wikis for professional conferences such as ALA Chicago 2005 and Internet Librarian 2007. "I have found a lot of good uses for wikis," she explains. "I'm all about librarians collaborating and sharing ideas to benefit the profession." Meredith is also the author of a blog called *Information Wants to Be Free* (http://meredith.wolfwater .com/wordpress/) in which she writes about her professional interests. In addition, she participates in other social networks such as FriendFeed, Flickr, and Facebook. "While these are not directly related to my job," she says, "I think they have a positive impact on my work as they keep me engaged with professional issues and have helped me build up an excellent professional network that I can rely on when I need help with a particular work project." At work, Meredith maintains two blogs that are used to dynamically display news content in various places on the website using RSS and JavaScript. Her library also uses a wiki as a content management system to publish and update subject guides.

In 2006 Meredith was named a *Library Journal* "Mover and Shaker" for her skills at serving patrons and other librarians while "playing with technology." "Who would have ever thought I'd get an award for playing?" she jokes.

Before becoming a librarian, Meredith earned a master of social work degree from Florida State University (FSU) and worked as a child and family therapist. In that position she provided in-home family counseling and assessment to low-income families in crisis. "I loved working with my clients," she says, "but funding limitations often prevented us from being effective. It was stressful to want to help people and be severely limited in the sort of help I could offer." She began looking for the sort of career where she could help people in a more concrete way. Having always loved libraries and the "detective work" involved with research, she realized that librarianship was a natural fit. She earned her master of library and information science degree from FSU. Her first professional position was as the distance learning librarian in the

Kreitzberg Library. After three years she was promoted to her current position as head of instructional initiatives.

When asked how she became a "tech geek," Meredith confesses that she never did much with technology until she was in library school. "I became drawn to technology then because of the things I was reading about in blogs. Once I started blogging myself, I became even more interested and began trying out some of the interesting new technologies that were becoming available, like screencasting and co-browsing software. Most of what I know about technology I've learned through trying things out and (more often than not) breaking them a few times. I don't think I have any particular aptitude for technologies—just a lot of interest."

In library school, she took as many technology courses as she could. The two she found most useful were on web design and usability. "The usability course really helped me to think about what it is that contributes to a good or bad user experience, and that has definitely influenced my work a great deal," she says. "I learned basic HTML skills from the web design course and then continued practicing and incorporating new skills on my own."

To keep up with technology, Meredith takes advantage of free professional development opportunities available online. She reads professional journals (both scholarly and trade) and attends one national and one local conference per year. She attends other conferences by virtue of the fact that she is often invited to be a guest speaker, and her travel fees are paid by the sponsoring organization. She is a member of the American Library Association, the Association of College and Research Libraries, and the Library and Information Technology Association.

What she finds most useful for keeping up, however, are social networking tools. "I keep up with around 200 blogs that cover topics related to technology, libraries, education, or any combination thereof," she says. "I read them through my RSS reader, which keeps me from having to visit each individual blog to see if there's new content. Blogs are excellent because they provide the timeliest discussions of what people are working on. I also use sites like Twitter and FriendFeed as professional development tools. Lots of librarians are on these microblogging sites, and people often write about what they're working on at their library. It's a great opportunity to find out what's happening on the bleeding edge as well as to get help from other librarians in your network."

Meredith holds that there are two main reasons why social networking is so important to our profession. First, "social networking tools offer us the unprecedented ability to connect and build community with our patrons online." She says that libraries use social networking tools to collect local knowledge, disseminate information, get feedback, create a public forum, create learning communities, and provide library ser-vices wherever the patrons are. "When providing services to our patrons using social networking tools," she says, "it's critical that we understand how our patrons actually use these tools so that we don't violate their privacy or create something that simply won't get used." She feels that libraries are doing a much better job these days of being more responsive to the needs of their users and in providing seamless, 24/7 services.

The second reason social networking is important relates to how librarians use these tools for professional networking. "Social technologies are amazing professional networking tools," she says. "They essentially allow you to build up an international professional network, full of other librarians who are knowledgeable and passion-ate about what they do. When I look at my list of friends in Facebook, I see a list of people who are experts in just about every area of our professional work. Librarians can make important contacts through social networking that they can rely on for help in the future; whether it's help with a project at work or help in finding a job."

Meredith stresses that if you are interested in a career similar to hers, "don't simply rely on library school to teach you everything you need to know." She recommends taking the initiative and getting involved professionally, networking, learning new technologies, and doing things that get you noticed. Having the requisite skills is important, but it is often not enough to get you the job. "I got my first job out of library school because I tried out new technologies and wrote about them," she says. "I pursued professional development and networking opportunities and, through all that, made it clear to my employer that I was someone who was really passionate about the profession. Most libraries like to see someone who is a go-getter and who has a real love of what they do."

For more information about Meredith, visit the "about me" portion of her blog at http://meredith.wolfwater.com/wordpress/about-me/.

SARAH HOUGHTON-JAN

Digital Futures Manager for San José Public Library, San Rafael, California

"Technology in librarianship is all about change, constantly new, and therefore constantly interesting."

SARAH HOUGHTON-JAN, a self-proclaimed librarian and technology expert rolled into one, is popularly known as the "Librarian in Black" in the world of librarianship blogs. The blog (www.librarianinblack.net) is a one-stop shop for all librarians and library staff who have an interest in technology. In the site's "About" section, Sarah states, "The site was born out of my displeasure at having to wade through dozens of websites, blogs, and RSS feeds related to librarianship, technology, webmastery, and current issues to find those few posts that applied to me as a Tech Librarian." The name of the blog can be attributed to the library patrons at Sarah's day job, who routinely identify her as "that tall librarian who always wears black."

At the San José Public Library, Sarah is the digital futures manager. In this position, she is responsible for the library's web presences, including the library's website, WebOPAC, intranet, and extended web presence through sites such as WiFi Directories, Yelp, and Facebook. She manages three staff members and is involved with electronic resources as well as virtual reference.

Day to day, much of her time is spent in meetings for various committees, work groups, teams, and task forces. She also spends a lot of time answering e-mail messages, working with vendors, and helping to usher projects and recommendations for change through the committee structure of their joint library. The San José Public Library is unique in that it shares its main location, and much of its administration, with the San José State University Library. This makes for an interesting collaborative partnership. "This is the most challenging and unique feature of my job," Sarah says. "I am not aware of any other technology managers that work in a combined public/ university library environment."

Sarah's primary patrons are the nearly million residents of San José. The library's users are typical of a large multiethnic urban environment. "We have speakers of nearly every language in our city," she says, "and very large populations of Vietnamese, Cantonese, and Spanish speakers." To reach out to these population groups, Sarah and her staff offer Spanish, Vietnamese, and Chinese versions of the library website. "Education levels vary widely. We are in the heart of Silicon Valley, so we also have a lot of users who are very technologically proficient and therefore expect a lot from our library's technological services. Our group is simply so dynamic, so diverse, and so interesting."

When she was young, Sarah's mother told her she would be a librarian. The idea, however, did not appeal to her at first. She followed her knack for the field of literature by pursuing a B.A. in English literature and language at the University of Illinois at Urbana-Champaign. She then earned an M.A. in literature, with a specialization in Irish literature, from Washington State University. Halfway through her master's program she realized that what she liked about her field was the research and the analysis of sources, not the writing of papers or the esoteric arguments about literary theory. "I decided then to do what others in my life had been pointing me toward all along—to get a degree in library and information science," she says. She headed back to the University of Illinois at Urbana-Champaign to enroll in library school.

"Despite the fact that I worked in several non-librarian positions in libraries during my schooling," she adds, "I fear that I went into the field quite ill-informed, believing that most librarians did research and focused on reference services. Once in library school, however, I quickly realized that the profession was so vast and variable that I could do just about anything I wanted." She began with a focus on rare books and digitization of such materials for enhanced access. She was pointed toward technology by the supervisor of an assistantship position at the Undergraduate Library, who handed over the ownership of part of the library's website to Sarah. She then started to refocus her education by taking every tech-based class available, such as Online Information Systems and Information Architecture.

After graduating, she got a position as the electronic services librarian at the Marin County Free Library in San Rafael, California. While there, she worked in four key areas: website design and maintenance, technology training, electronic resources research and purchasing, and virtual reference services. "I learned on the job to expand my skills and fell in love with the technology side of librarianship then and there," she says. "That area of the field was relatively new, especially when it came to web technologies, e-content, and technology training. I've been learning nonstop since then, packing away useful tools, techniques, sites, services, and strategies for future use and sharing with others. I think that I will stay in the technology side of librarianship."

Next, Sarah worked for two years for the San Mateo County Library as its web services manager, where she was responsible for the same key areas but also had staff to help. She began in her current position in 2007. "With each successive job, my responsibilities increased and I now spend more time managing rather than actually doing the projects themselves," she says. "I miss getting my hands into the website, creating final products, something tangible that I can say I was responsible for. But managing the work helps to grease the wheels to allow others to get that work done, so I take satisfaction in that."

In addition to her regular "day job," Sarah is a consultant instructor for Infopeople. This is a federally funded statewide program that offers a wide variety of training to those who work in California libraries. Sarah is qualified to speak to libraries and other organizations about a variety of library and technology topics, such as accessibility and usability, blogging, database marketing and training, e-books, e-music, e-video, e-resource statistical analysis, filtering, gaming, information architecture, online marketing, podcasting, project management, social networking, technology competencies, virtual reference, virtual worlds, and website design. In addition to the consulting she does for Infopeople, Sarah has been invited to speak internationally at live and online events for libraries and other institutions.

Sarah is very active in social networking through wikis, blogs, and other venues. "They definitely tie in with my day job," she explains. "The skills I learn using Facebook, for example, help me to create a good Facebook presence for the library. The experience I have with running a blog for several years helps me with creating best practices for our library bloggers. I think it is important that every library has librarians who are involved with social networking. It is important to tap this new resource, this new opportunity for outreach to customers." In addition, Sarah reads about 500 RSS feeds from various sources in order to keep up with technology. She reads e-mail newsletters about technology and reference topics and belongs to a dozen library electronic discussion lists. She maintains memberships in the American Library Association, the Public Library Association, the American Society for Information Science and Technology, and the Library and Information Technology Association.

Sarah was recently named a *Library Journal* "2009 Mover and Shaker" for her trend-spotting accomplishments. She is constantly on the watch for new trends and serves on LITA's Top Technology Trends Committee. She tracks cutting-edge publications to keep up with recent "buzz" topics and how they affect libraries.

To those interested in a similar career, Sarah advises getting a good undergraduate background in business, management, or computer science. "Then it's on to library school where I would recommend taking as many classes on technology as possible, but also balancing that out with classes on other library services, such as children's and teen services, reference, cataloging, circulation, etc. I would also recommend being willing to start in a non-tech-related librarian position in order to gain experience. You can likely volunteer for different tech projects and get some experience under your belt to make yourself more marketable as a 'technology' librarian."

"Technology has simply been the focus of my career," Sarah concludes. "I would probably be a reference librarian, scared to lose my job right now, if I had not focused on technology or if technology and web services had not risen so quickly to their current heights."

If you'd like to learn more about Sarah and her professional and personal activities, visit www.librarianinblack.net.

LORI BELL

Director of Innovation, Alliance Library System, East Peoria, Illinois

"Librarians need to stay on top of social networking tools. They need to be where the users are."

Lori Bell works for an organization whose primary patrons are other libraries. The Alliance Library System (ALS), headquartered in East Peoria, Illinois, is a "multi-type library system" that serves 258 school, special, academic, and public libraries in a 14,000-square-mile area in central and west-central Illinois. ALS, one of nine such multi-type library systems in Illinois, provides continuing education sessions, consulting assistance, material delivery, resource sharing, grant-writing assistance, and collaborative grant management. The organization also supports the Talking Books program (a service for the visually impaired), manages the automated library catalog, and teaches librarians how to do their job better.

As the director of innovation at ALS, Lori is responsible for writing and managing grant projects and helping members in writing grants. Currently she is involved with the management of five grant projects, as well as several others that are at different stages of the grant-writing process. She assists members in keeping up with trends and in writing grants to fund trend-related projects. She is also involved with various training sessions as well as the Talking Books program.

One of Lori's biggest projects is the management of the Second Life Library (now known as the Alliance Virtual Library). Second Life is a 3-D, interactive virtual world. It is a complete community with businesses, recreation, buildings, services, and cultural programs (see Rhonda Trueman's entry next in this chapter for further discussion of virtual worlds). Not only is Second Life used for entertainment by its over five million avatars, it has developed to the point that it is being used to facilitate meetings and dialogue among organizations and support groups. It's also being used for higher education purposes such as distance education. Recognizing the importance of incorporating library services into such an active virtual community, ALS got its foot in the virtual door in 2006 with its Second Life Library project. After starting out with one rented building and a small plot of land in Second Life, Lori and a team of volunteers have managed to expand the project into an "Info Island Archipelago" consisting of multiple "islands" or simulators. There are over fifty library islands and partners in the archipelago, including Info Islands I and II, Health Info Island, Eduisland, Cybrary City, and many others (visit http://infoisland.org). ALS also maintains two virtual projects: adult Second Life and Teen Second Life (for ages 13–17), which provide a full array of services.

This strong library presence within Second Life results in many types of services: reference (virtual or by e-mail); collections grouped by topic (web resources and Second Life formatted books); book discussions and author visits; training in the use of library resources and how to do things in Second Life; weekly programs on an array of topics; and exhibits (coordinated by libraries and museums).

"The original purpose of Second Life Library was to see if people/avatars would use library services in a virtual world," Lori says. "We found that they would and do. Over 5,000 avatars visit the Info Island per day. I had no idea it would take off as well as it has. I think people are using it for a variety of personal and professional reasons: to network, to offer library collections and services, to provide instructional support for academic classes meeting in Second Life, and for attending conferences and educational events." Many librarians who volunteer for the Alliance Virtual Library project feel that this is the new frontier. Virtual worlds can be used to attract new users, provide library services 24/7, and meet colleagues from around the world.

In 2007 the Alliance Second Life Library Program received the American Library Association's Library of the Future Award. The program developers, including Lori Bell, received recognition for their "groundbreaking work in the development of a 3-D virtual environment, for forging new partnerships within the virtual world, and for providing programs, services, and materials to the more than 1.3 million residents who inhabit Second Life."[6] Despite its success, Lori says that there are many challenges involved with the Alliance Virtual Library project. First of all, funding and sustainability are key issues. This is why Lori must constantly pursue grant opportunities to support Second Life Library activities. Believe it or not, it does cost money to provide virtual resources. Second, supporting a large project using volunteer staffing is challenging. The volunteers are dedicated, but they are spread worldwide, and coordination can sometimes be difficult. In addition, there is a steep learning curve for working in a virtual world; it requires a whole new set of skills. Finally, the work is highly addictive and takes lots of time. "Not everyone understands that when you are in Second Life you are working, but you might be having fun, too," Lori explains. "Sometimes convincing bosses of this is challenging."

Lorelei Junot is the name of Lori's professional avatar in Second Life. "She represents me at work and participates in all the Second Life Library activities," Lori says. "Everyone knows who she is and they know about my real-life information. I also have an anonymous personal avatar who does the fun stuff like exploring and dancing."

Recently, Lori coedited a book along with her "virtual" colleague, Rhonda Trueman (see Rhonda's interview next in this chapter). The book, released in October 2008 by Information Today, Inc., is called *Virtual Worlds, Real Libraries: Librarians and Educators in Second Life and Other Multi-User Virtual Environments* and is designed to help libraries and schools recognize the importance of virtual environments and consider ways of getting involved. The editors and twenty-four contributors recount their experiences in working together in Second Life to offer library services in the virtual environment. Lori and Rhonda met through the Second Life Library project and remained "virtual" friends until they met in person at a conference. Since then, they have collaborated on a number of projects, the most recent one being the book.

Lori received her master of library and information science degree from the University of Illinois. She also has an advanced certificate in distance learning from Western Illinois University. "I became interested in a career in libraries when I worked as an undergraduate student in government documents in the university library," she says. "I have had a variety of positions—children's services, public services, extension services. I worked at a state library and several library systems.

"I have always been interested in technology," Lori says. "It is challenging and exciting to try to discover what the 'next big thing' will be, and trying to keep up with trends and how they might affect libraries." She keeps up with technology by taking continuing education courses, participating in blogs, attending conferences, reading articles, and—of course—keeping in contact with colleagues through the Second Life project. She is a member of the Illinois Library Association and the American Library Association, and she serves as the co-convener of the ALA Virtual Communities and Libraries Membership Interest Group.

"It is exciting to be a librarian today," she concludes. "Technology has influenced my career in that each job I have had, I have made use of technology to try new services in whatever area I am working on. New librarians should try a lot of different things, try new technologies, and keep on top of trends."

RHONDA BRIDGES TRUEMAN

Head of Reference, Johnson and Wales University, Charlotte, North Carolina
Director of Library Services and Resources, Alliance Virtual Library (Second Life)

*"Second Life is a virtual world that is far from a game;
it is a way to create both a 3-D world and a community."*

VIRTUAL WORLDS have opened up new and exciting avenues for information delivery. In these high-tech times when lives are built around technology, electronics, and social networking venues, virtual worlds enable librarians to reach groups of people, such as the younger generation, who would normally be unreachable through traditional library services. Librarians have already recognized that a large percentage of Internet users are engaged or will soon be engaged in some form of virtual world activity. They have taken steps to ensure that traditional library services such as reference, teaching, collections, exhibits, and discussion groups are applied successfully in the virtual environment.

Virtual worlds are three-dimensional, interactive digital worlds that are normally web-based. Each virtual world—also called a multi-user virtual environment—is created by its "residents." To become a resident of a virtual world, a person would normally need to download a viewer and then create a virtual persona called an avatar. A person's avatar is only limited by one's imagination. Avatars may take the form of people, animals, robots, or even imaginary creatures like dragons. Once their avatar is created, people can then choose from thousands of unique clothing, hair, and fashion accessories found in resident-owned shops. Avatars can walk, "teleport," or even fly to thousands of 3-D locations. They are able to use voice and text chat to communicate with other avatars and real people around the world. Some virtual worlds are game-based, but most feature unlimited freedom as in "real life." Users can explore thousands of places and enjoy services and events such as live music performances, interactive exhibits, shopping centers, fashion shows, and nightclubs. Avatars may also purchase goods and services, buy land, find jobs, and earn virtual money.

Rhonda Trueman is deeply involved with the popular virtual world called Second Life (http://secondlife.com). In particular, she works with Alliance Virtual Library, which is a project that encompasses all library services within Second Life. As the director of library services and resources, she oversees the operations of the library "sims," or simulators. There are five different library sims in Second Life: Info Island, Info Island International, Imagination Island, Infotainment Island, and Illumination

Island (each island equals about sixteen acres of land in real-life real estate). These library sims represent a huge collaborative effort among volunteer librarians from around the world. The sims offer traditional library services such as resources, collections, exhibits, online pathfinders, and varied events such as book discussions, all of which are coordinated by librarians who volunteer their time to the Alliance Virtual Library project. There are even reference services available eighty hours per week. Rhonda is responsible for coordinating all of these volunteer projects and services.

Rhonda (also known as Abbey Zenith in Second Life) devotes about twenty volunteer hours per week to her "virtual" job with Second Life and finds it very rewarding professionally. "You get to meet people from all over the globe, in all levels of librarianship," she says, "and you are able to get to know them and collaborate with them." The work also enables her to share professional information with librarians and discuss emerging issues. "It's like a big conference that never ends."

Rhonda became involved with Second Life in 2006, when she discovered what was then known as Second Life Library 2.0 and jumped at the chance to volunteer. "I began by doing small things," she says, "like leading tours, helping people with Second Life skills, building and developing library areas and resources." In the summer of 2006 she was asked to become head of collections for the project, and as the project grew she became director of operations of the Second Life Library. Over the next few years the project grew exponentially and she assumed her current role as director of library services and resources.

Recently, Rhonda edited a book along with her "virtual" colleague, Lori Bell (see Lori's interview earlier in this chapter). The book, released in October 2008 by Information Today, Inc., is called *Virtual Worlds, Real Libraries: Librarians and Educators in Second Life and Other Multi-User Virtual Environments* and is designed to help libraries and schools recognize the importance of virtual environments and consider ways of getting involved. The editors and twenty-four contributors recount their experiences in working together in Second Life to offer library services in the virtual environment.

Most of the volunteer librarians involved with the Alliance Virtual Library project also have "day jobs." The same is true for Rhonda. In her "real job" she is head of reference at Johnson and Wales University (JWU), a nonprofit, private university offering undergraduate and graduate degree programs in business, hospitality, culinary arts, technology, and education. When she first began at JWU, she was responsible for managing the periodicals and was liaison for the College of Business. Later she accepted the additional responsibilities of managing the library's website and tracking library statistics. In her current position she continues as liaison for the College of Business, manages the Reference Department, and supervises fifteen work-study students. Building on her interest in social networking, she recently implemented a library blog to facilitate faculty and library staff communication on campus, introduced the use of Meebo to provide instant message reference services, and created a Facebook page for the library.

Rhonda's daily responsibilities include working with the work-study students to provide circulation services to patrons; searching for books, DVDs, and other materials to enhance the library's business, reference, and popular fiction collections; working with College of Business faculty on research projects; and providing instructional sessions in library research for the business classes. She also looks for professional development opportunities for the reference staff and has implemented a program of selected readings on reference issues and trends.

"The most challenging aspect of my position," says Rhonda, "is expanding my role from reference librarian to head of reference. This is the first time we have had this role at our library, because we are small. I have researched job descriptions to see what duties are carried out by other heads of reference at other institutions and am adapting them to what is possible within our framework."

Rhonda shares common ground with all JWU librarians. The main university is located in Providence, Rhode Island. Each regional campus, including the Charlotte campus, has a library director and similar staffing (up to five librarians). "We all take turns working reference, we all participate in instruction, and several of us help with cataloging duties as time allows," she says. "It is a wonderful, collaborative experience for each regional library; we collaborate with each other as part of a larger system of libraries."

Rhonda feels that the ability to work as a team player is an important skill for librarians at her institution. "With a small staff it is important that we become cross-trained to a certain extent and that we are able to help each other with our duties. As an academic librarian the most important skills are being able to listen to a student and ascertain their needs when they are sometimes not sure themselves, then to be able to instruct that student to successfully find the materials they need, whether in the catalog, in the databases, or elsewhere. We enable student growth not by giving them the answer but by showing them how to find it."

As is common with many in the field, Rhonda did not at first set out to be a librarian. Her background is in business, and she worked for many years as office manager for corporations ranging in size from 8 to 40 people. "My technology interests led me to the development of websites for these organizations and under contract for other organizations," she says. After finishing a B.A. in English from the University of

North Carolina at Charlotte, she continued along the business career path with added responsibilities in writing, marketing, and training coordination. From there, she went on to event management, becoming the director of meetings and conferences for a trade association.

"This career path was successful and rewarding, but never planned, and never what I felt I really wanted to be doing," Rhonda says. "A friend that was in the LIS program at the University of North Carolina Greensboro contacted me and said that she thought this was a perfect fit for me. It was one of those 'lightbulb' moments and I realized that yes, this was what I wanted to do and that I should go for it. In just over one year I completed my degree and shortly thereafter accepted my current position with Johnson and Wales University."

Since technology is a special interest of hers, Rhonda does not find it very difficult to keep up with technological changes in the field. She reads library publications, takes continuing education courses, and attends conferences. She is a member of the American Library Association, the Association of College and Research Libraries, the Reference and User Services Association, the North Carolina Library Association, and a local organization called Metrolina Library Association. "In addition, my involvement with Second Life has placed me within a circle of colleagues who are very astute professionals," she adds. "We freely share information and instruction on changing technology."

For Rhonda, being a librarian today means service to the community by providing assistance in locating and accessing information. "Today there is a much broader scope of information delivery, and part of my job is to be aware of the changes in technology that enable me to find and provide information. Since I have become a librarian, Web 2.0 services have exploded, making keeping up with technology and being comfortable using new technology a requirement for the profession."

Social networking is key to Rhonda's philosophy of librarianship. "Community is such a big part of what we do as librarians, even in academic librarianship," she explains. "It's important to make the library indispensable as a gathering place where like-minded people, students, faculty, staff, and residents can explore and access information, meet with each other, hold discussions, hear stories, and attend classes. This transforms the library into more than just a depository for materials, more than its electronic databases, more than the sum of what makes up a library. It becomes a tool for social networking and community building."

DAVID LEE KING

Digital Branch and Services Manager, Topeka and Shawnee County Public Library, Topeka, Kansas

*"I participate in social networks to experiment,
then to bring the 'good stuff' back to my library."*

A SHORT five years ago, the term *digital library branch* would have left many people puzzled. A library branch with no walls? No physical location? What's up with that? David King of Topeka, Kansas, can answer that question, because he is the digital branch and services manager of the Topeka and Shawnee County Public Library. He succinctly defines a digital branch as "an online place where patrons can actually do stuff—find materials, get answers, interact with library staff, and interact with the local community."

David is responsible for managing the library's Information Technology Department, managing the library website, and spearheading digital initiatives. As part of the library's management team, he is also responsible for long-range departmental planning. "My primary clientele are library staff," he says, but he also serves the information technology needs of a wide range of library patrons—from those with special needs to professors with advanced degrees.

David's daily routine varies greatly, but usually includes periodic e-mail communication, the reading of RSS feeds to stay current, participation in meetings of various types, and dealing with problems as they occur. "I usually get the 'escalated' problems that need a manager's input," he says. A large portion of his time is spent helping the library staff navigate the digital branch, which might involve such things as showing staff how to write a better blog post or how to find a tool that works in Facebook.

"Our digital branch has been the most exciting part of my job," David says. "Most libraries aren't thinking of their website as a library branch. Thinking about the implications of that and what I could do really excited me. And I think that's a pretty unique feature of my job. If you remove the 'digital' part of my title, I'm really a branch manager! I deal with collections, facility, staff, and maintenance issues—just online in our digital branch."

Before becoming a librarian, David tried his hand at a variety of jobs. He worked as a disc jockey, a "pizza delivery dude," a construction worker, a customer service representative, a musician, and a freelance recording engineer. How did librarianship come into the picture? He received his undergraduate degree at William Jewell College in Liberty, Missouri, with a double major in religion and communication. He often "hung out" with musicians, and after college he and his wife moved to Nashville, Tennessee, so that he could try his hand at being a musician. Eventually he realized that it was difficult to make a good living in the music industry, so he bought a career guidance book called *What Color Is Your Parachute?* The book steered him toward the realization that he had really enjoyed spending time at the library and doing research during his undergraduate years. "Presto! I realized that a career in librarian-ship might just be interesting," he says. He enrolled in the library science program at the University of Tennessee at Knoxville and completed his master's degree there.

After graduating, David served as an electronic services librarian at the University of Southern Mississippi and as the biomedical/reference librarian at the University of Kansas Medical Center. His public library experience began in Kansas City, Missouri, where he served as the assistant information technology services director and later as the acting director of information technology services at the Kansas City Public Library. In the fall of 2006 he accepted his current position at the Topeka and Shawnee County Public Library.

Technology is key to David's position. "My job wouldn't exist without technology," he says. Social networking also plays a large role in his professional work. "Pretty much my forty-hour workweek is spent connecting with colleagues and staff on the computer and on the Web." He maintains that social networking is really about people connecting with people, while using technology to do so. He participates on Twitter, Facebook, MySpace, YouTube, Last.fm, Flickr, and Second Life. What he gathers from experimenting with these social networking outlets he brings into his day job for practical application.

David's own website (www.davidleeking.com) focuses on professional discussions about technology and website topics. The "About" portion of the website states, "I create, write, think, and speak about library websites and emerging digital technol-ogy. This website reflects those topics. I tend toward library website stuff—manag-ing, marketing, experimenting, usability, and planning. Sometimes I stray into other related-yet-cool (translation: fun) topics, like videoblogging, experience design and planning, and Web 2.0/Library 2.0 topics. Basically, anything in my head on any given day that's somehow related to libraries, digital technology, and websites." His website also incorporates a very active blog.

David recently celebrated the publication of his first book, *Designing the Digital Experience* (CyberAge Books, 2008). The book is a guide to creating useful and easily navigable websites using "experience design" tools and techniques.

It is obvious that David keeps up with changing technology. But even a "techie" needs to work at it. To keep up, he reads blogs and RSS feeds and attends conferences.

He also networks with colleagues. "Most important," he says, "is that I experiment. The only way to keep up with changing technology is to get your hands on a new thing and play with it; basically immersing yourself in the product, tool, or service and seeing how it relates to your organization and customers." In addition, he is a member of various professional organizations where he sees his role as helping with change on a broad scale.

"Simply stated," David says, "my career has been an outgrowth of my willingness to embrace change and learn new technology. In the last seven or eight years, technology has changed dramatically. The Web has morphed from primarily information and access to primarily a mix of content and connections. That is a huge change." Certain skills, he maintains, are important for librarians in positions involving the Web or technology: the ability to deal with and embrace change; the ability to learn new technological tools quickly; the ability to see how a new tool or service could relate to a library community; the ability to scan the horizon; being able to communicate well in person, in print, in e-mail, on blogs, and on video; and being able to see and communicate the "big picture" to staff.

David maintains that today's librarian needs to focus not on the patron that comes through the door, but on the potential patrons in the greater community. When librarians do focus on patrons coming through the door, they need to focus on more than one door. "There is a physical door, and there are many digital doors, including a website, a comment box, a Facebook page, or a Google search.

"Immerse yourself in social networks," says David. "Be open to change, constantly 'play' with new tools and services, and learn how to be patient."

If you'd like to learn more about David and his professional and personal activities, visit www.davidleeking.com.

MICHAEL PORTER

Communications Manager, WebJunction
Presenting, Writing, and Consulting via Libraryman.com, Seattle, Washington

*"It is such a blessing to work for an organization
you really believe in and feel good about."*

MICHAEL PORTER has difficulty finding one title that accurately describes himself. This is because he is a man of many talents and interests. His blog profile states that he is "a librarian, blogger, presenter, technology fan, author, and PEZ collector." All of his interests—except perhaps the PEZ collection!—are unified by his strong belief that "the public library is a vibrant societal and cultural institution of immeasurable value to society, democracy, and mankind."

Michael is the communications manager at WebJunction (www.webjunction.org/ home/), a nonprofit organization whose mission is to promote learning for all library staff by providing open, affordable online learning communities. WebJunction's website states, "Our vision is to be the place where the library profession gathers to build the knowledge, skills and support we need to power relevant, vibrant libraries. We value community, collaboration, and support for lifelong learning. These values ensure that all libraries—regardless of size, type, or geographic location—can effectively use and share resources toward common goals."

Michael is part of a small team that has helped more than 50,000 library staff build job skills needed to meet the challenges of today's libraries. "My job is pretty diverse," he says. "It is a small organization and we all tend to wear a lot of hats. Things change depending on what needs to get done, what events are happening in library land, and what grants we are working on. Usually, though, about half of my time is spent dealing with marketing and communications. Because we are a part of OCLC, I get to work with their creative team on things like marketing, outreach, communications, and campaigns, and this is very interesting work. You have to be very organized and attend a lot of meetings to do this work, but you get to work with good people and be creative while producing some really useful things like fliers, publications, and ads.

"I am so fortunate to work with an amazing group of colleagues at WebJunction," Michael says. "Everyone plays a part in seeking out and creating huge amounts of content, preparing presentations, and developing relationships with libraries and other organizations in the United States and around the world. The team is really what makes it all happen, and I am just a part of that."

A big part of Michael's job involves working with online social tools to get the word out about events, publications, courses, and other fresh content. He is also involved with representing WebJunction at library conferences and events. "Every year," he says, "we attend the American Library Association's Annual and Midwinter conferences and host several WebJunction events at each. Most of us present regularly at these meetings. I keep tabs on the presentations and make sure logistics are in place. This keeps us very busy around the Annual and Midwinter conference dates. Despite all the work, it ends up being a lot of fun."

Michael is also involved with compiling a weekly media report. "This report has evolved in recent years as technology and social engagement online have evolved," he says. "We keep track of activity on social sites related to WebJunction, to be sure we are 'getting the word out' about what we do. We track things like blog mentions, web mentions, print mentions, and Facebook and Twitter activity related to WebJunction. We keep statistics about our web traffic, in-person event attendance, and webinar attendance to give us a clear picture of our institutional reach and areas for improvement. We also use those numbers on our grant reports, and our monthly and yearly reports. In my job, there is definitely plenty to do, but it's great work and I am grateful to work for an organization that does so much to help libraries and library staff."

Outside of his work at WebJunction, Michael is often invited to give presentations on different library issues at conferences or to individual library staffs. "I usually go on about one trip a month to present at a staff day, conference, or event," he explains. "It took many years of presenting, writing, working, and slogging it out before I was able to get gigs like this, but if you are interested in public speaking, have a knack for it, and really work at it, there are many opportunities to do this kind of work. Of course, to be a sought-after presenter, you'll need to do a lot of extra work, not only to grow as a public speaker, but also to become an expert on the things you will talk about. Early on I started talking about online social tools, gadgets, and their intersection with the future of libraries. As we've seen, those topics continue to unfold for libraries in fascinating ways. And I love learning about them! I am able to apply what I learn to my 'real' job."

In 2009 Michael was selected as a *Library Journal* "Mover and Shaker." In 2010 he was elected to the American Library Association's governing Council Board, where he coauthored a resolution that takes a stand for "an effective electronic content access and distribution infrastructure that facilitates access to electronic content of all types for all library users." He also writes the "Internet Spotlight" column for *Public Libraries* magazine with his friend and colleague, David Lee King (see David's interview earlier in this chapter).

In recent months, Michael has been working on starting a new nonprofit organization called Library Renewal that will help libraries decide how best to get electronic content into the hands of library users. "This is a complicated, evolving issue," he says, "but in my estimation it is the most important issue facing libraries today and in the next three decades. I encourage readers of this book to take a look at Library Renewal and get involved with promoting libraries as conduits for electronic content access in the coming decades."

Ever since Michael created his first web page back in 1995, he has always felt comfortable with technology. "I loved playing around on the Web in those early days and would often try to imagine what the implications would be for day-to-day life and library services because of these new tools." In 2000 he created a website called "Libraryman" which morphed into the *Libraryman* blog in 2003 (www.libraryman .com/blog/), which is quite popular to this day. Michael uses Twitter and Facebook to communicate with friends and colleagues. "I've made a conscious decision to use these tools mostly for professional purposes," he says. "Most days you'll find me sharing resources, links, ideas, or questions. You know, if you read this book ten or twenty years after it has been published, you can just replace 'Twitter' or 'Facebook' with whatever folks are using (hopefully through a library service) and look for Michael Porter, Libraryman."

Michael is responsible for creating a few notable online groups that continue to have an active membership. "I started them, nurtured them, and they took off because of the great people in library land." These include the "Libraries and Librarians" group on Flickr, which purports to be the largest, most diverse collection of library and librarian-related images in the world; the "365 Library Days" on Flickr; the "Libraries and Librarians" group on Facebook; and the "Libraries and Librarians Guild" in World of Warcraft.

Michael has a B.F.A. in painting and sculpture from Indiana University. Before enrolling in graduate school, he worked for nearly ten years at the Allen County Public Library in Fort Wayne, Indiana, where he started as an entry-level clerk checking books in and out and was later promoted to a job in the Children's Department. "The Children's Department was run by an amazing librarian, Mary Voors," he says. "Mary demanded hard work from all her staff, but she was also approachable and encouraging, and she eventually convinced me that I could get my M.L.S., become a librarian, and do things to help my own career as well as the community at large through work in the field.

"In the Children's Department I could directly see the incredibly powerful, real-life impact that libraries have on individual lives," Michael continues. "I knew dozens of children who clearly used the library as a safe haven and respite from their clearly unpleasant home lives. It was an honor to help secure that safe physical space for them, and at the same time offer them services to help nurture their minds, knowing that this growth was certain to be a key for them to break the unpleasant cycle of their home lives. It was also encouraging to see that most families visiting the library were good, thoughtful community members who brought their families to the library as part of their intellectual and civic engagement." During that time, Michael became friends with a librarian named Steve Miller, who demonstrated what it was like to be a "modern" librarian. "Between Steve and my supervisor, Mary, along with a promotion to reference librarian at a busy branch, I finally felt like getting that advanced degree was clearly the right decision."

Michael enrolled in the M.L.S. program at Indiana University (IU) and immediately became active in the ALA's Student Chapter at IU. His election as president of that organization was a critically important professional experience for him. "I would never have imagined that I could put myself out there and be successful," he says. "It is amazing what opportunities unfold if you just try. You have to be willing to follow through, but if you just ask, and try, things really can start to become possible." Michael's experience as president of the Student Chapter opened several doors for him later in his career.

After graduate school, Michael moved to Seattle to work for the Bill and Melinda Gates Foundation U.S. Library Program as a "public access computing trainer." In that position, he spent four years on the road—two out of every three weeks—traveling the country, working in thirty-two states and visiting libraries, training library staff how to use computers and the Internet more effectively. "This job was a rare, stunning, and simply amazing experience," he says. "Seeing hundreds of libraries—mostly in small or medium-sized towns that most folks haven't heard of—and seeing over and over again the benefits that libraries bring to communities was incredible and career shaping. After seeing that, I've really had no other choice but to do all I can to help libraries and library staff succeed and thrive."

To those just starting out in the field of librarianship, Michael says, "Don't accept being stuck in a job you don't like. Start over if you need to. Be smart. Be creative. Have fun. Play to your strengths. Work *hard*. Work *smart*. Realize that you can do more than you ever thought you could; you just have to try, try, try. I absolutely believe that it is critical that libraries not only just continue to exist, but become more stable, more vibrant, and even more useful. You will feel honored to be a part of all that."

Michael would like to share the following websites:

- www.libraryrenewal.org (the Library Renewal website)
- www.libraryman.com/blog/ (the *Libraryman* blog)

- http://twitter.com/libraryman/ (his Twitter page)
- www.facebook.com/Libraryman/ (his Facebook page)
- www.flickr.com/groups/librariesandlibrarians/ ("Libraries and Librarians" group on Flickr)
- http://wowlibraryguild.com ("Library Guild" on World of Warcraft)

NOTES

1. Linda Main, "Librarians: The Best Googlers in the World," in *The Portable MLIS: Insights from the Experts* (Westport, CT: Libraries Unlimited, 2008).
2. Michael Stephens, "Creating Conversations, Connections, and Community," *Library Technology Reports,* July/August 2006, 6–7.
3. Michael Stephens, "Putting Your Library 'Out There,'" *Library Technology Reports,* July/August 2006, 63–66.
4. Meredith Farkas, "Skills for the 21st Century Librarian," 2006, http://meredith.wolf water.com/wordpress/2006/07/17/skills-for-the-21st-century-librarian/.
5. Gabe Rios, "Top 10 Technology Trends Librarians Should Be Conversant With," 2007, http://medlibtechtrends.wordpress.com/2007/03/01/top-10-technology-trends-librarians -should-be-conversant-on-gabe-rios/.
6. American Library Association press release, "Alliance Library System Program Receives 2007 Library of the Future Award," 2007, www.ala.org/Template.cfm? Section=archive&template=/contentmanagement/contentdisplay.cfm&ContentID= 155771.

CHAPTER 3

LIBRARIANS AS TEACHERS AND COMMUNITY LIAISONS

LIBRARIANS ARE constantly teaching library users—to search online catalogs, for example, or to use databases and search engines, to navigate print and electronic resources, or to conduct a literature search or do basic research. In the twenty-first century, librarians are embracing teaching as a primary responsibility rather than just a peripheral duty. This trend is evidenced by the increase in volume of library position announcements with titles such as "Instruction Librarian," "User Education Librarian," or "Head of Education and Outreach." Teaching the skills that comprise "information literacy"—the ability to locate, analyze, evaluate, and use information effectively—is integral to the job of almost every librarian in any type of setting.[1]

If you are drawn to librarianship because you see yourself as an introvert and would rather not be involved with teaching or presenting, you might need to reevaluate. No longer can a librarian sit at his or her desk behind the safety of journals and books. Now more than ever, librarians are being asked to cross the boundaries of what used to be "technical services," "public services," or "systems." The responsibility of teaching is often what makes these "lines of demarcation" fuzzy. The trend of "librarians as teachers" is rapidly changing the profession so that nearly every librarian in an organization, particularly in an academic setting, is involved with teaching or instruction in some way.

This chapter spotlights the different types of teacher-librarians—from school library media specialists to educators in library and information science programs—and includes those involved in outreach or community liaison. Though not teachers in the traditional sense, librarians involved with community outreach are charged with the task of teaching the communities they serve about the resources and programs available to them through libraries. No matter what the setting or the job title, many believe that the most effective librarians are those who empower learners and who facilitate the teaching and learning process.[2]

ENVIRONMENTS

Public libraries. Public librarians have long been involved with teaching library literacy as well as with community outreach. Children's librarians, reference librarians, and even systems librarians are charged with various teaching and outreach programs. The overall goals are to empower library patrons with the ability to find and analyze information, and to match subsets of the user community with information most useful to them.

Academic libraries. Librarians in the academic setting are increasingly responsible for a variety of activities directly related to teaching and learning. The scope of those responsibilities has expanded in recent years to encompass instruction delivered within the library as well as across the campus or in online learning environments.[3]

School libraries. School librarians, or media specialists, must now add teaching to their extensive list of responsibilities. Though they have traditionally been responsible for teaching library literacy, teaching by librarians is now done more formally within school curriculums. School librarians tend to use the library as an outreach tool to instill library literacy, a curiosity for information, as well as a love of reading and literature in their students. They may teach reference and bibliographic skills—appropriate to each grade level—using tools such as games, worksheets, and electronic presentations.

Schools of library and information science. The faculty members employed at schools of library and information science (LIS) are teachers first and foremost. Their task is to arm library school students with the tools and skills needed to succeed in the practice of librarianship. Though they may still teach in traditional classroom settings, they are likely to be involved in distance education or the online teaching environment.

Other settings. Librarians in virtually any setting may be involved with teaching. Corporate librarians may offer seminars to clients on market research or competitive intelligence. Law librarians may teach classes to the general public on locating legal documents. Clinical medical librarians might teach physicians how to use a mobile device to search medical databases at the patient bedside. No matter the environment, teaching opens up entirely new avenues of responsibility for librarians.

SKILLS

Librarians need teaching and training skills as much as they need the more familiar and traditional skills such as reference work or cataloging. In 2007 the Association of College and Research Libraries published a list of "Standards for Proficiencies for Instruction Librarians and Coordinators."[4] Though established specifically for the academic librarian, these standards can be applied to librarians who serve as teachers or instructors in any environment. Listed below are the twelve main categories of skills found in the document:

- administrative skills
- assessment and evaluation skills
- communication skills
- curriculum knowledge
- information literacy integration skills
- instructional design skills
- leadership skills
- planning skills
- presentation skills
- promotion skills
- subject expertise
- teaching skills

EDUCATION AND TRAINING

Generally, most positions require a master's degree in library and information science from an ALA-accredited institution. School library media specialists must have teacher certification appropriate to the state in which they are employed. LIS faculty are often required to have a Ph.D. in library and information science or another area of study. Many librarians, especially in the academic setting, acquire teaching skills while on the job.

PROFESSIONAL ASSOCIATIONS

Below is a list of associations recommended by the various librarians "spotlighted" in this chapter:

- American Library Association (ALA)—www.ala.org
  - *American Association of School Librarians (AASL)* www.aasl.org
  - *Association of College and Research Libraries (ACRL)* www.acrl.org
- Association for Library and Information Science Education (ALISE)— www.alise.org
- Regional and local library associations

SPOTLIGHTS

MICHAEL STEPHENS

Assistant Professor, Graduate School of Library and Information Science, Dominican University, River Forest, Illinois

"If we adapt to change, we aren't thrown every time the world shifts."

MICHAEL STEPHENS is devoted to arming library school students with the tools and skills they need to succeed in practice. "One of the most important things we can do for students in library and information science education," he says, "is to show them that everything will change and that adaptation is key. I want my students to realize what great opportunities there are for libraries and librarians in this ever-changing world."

Michael holds a full-time tenure-track position as assistant professor at the Graduate School of Library and Information Science (GSLIS) at Dominican University. He teaches a variety of LIS courses, and even after several years, he finds it fulfilling. "We have two types of students—those returning for a second career and those fresh from their undergraduate degrees," he says. "This dynamic leads to useful discussions and sharing in the classroom. The fresh-from-the-undergrad students usually come from a liberal arts background. The returning students come from many professions. I've had an Intro to LIS class that had attorneys, teachers, graphic designers, computer programmers, and massage therapists in the mix—again, making for very interesting interactions in class. Seasoned folks from the workplace can share experiences while newly minted undergrads bring their perspectives and fresh ideas."

As with any position, being on the faculty of a library school has its challenges. Because Michael is on the tenure-track, he must balance the three core requirements of university faculty: teaching, service, and research. "I have to excel in all three to varying degrees," he says. "Dominican is mainly a teaching university—that's one of the most important things that brought me to the job. I wanted to focus on teaching. In the thick of working toward tenure, however, I have to balance committee work, university service, and keeping up with publishing.

"The most challenging thing about a teaching job in LIS," he continues, "is the fact that many people outside of our profession have no idea that a person needs a master's degree to be a professional librarian. It can be disheartening when someone says, 'Oh, I didn't know you had to go to school for that.' But I often use it as a way to educate people about what librarians do and the impact we have on the future."

In the publishing arena, Michael is certainly productive. He is the author of *The Library Internet Trainer's Toolkit* (Neal-Schuman, 2001) and two ALA Library Technology Reports on Web 2.0, and he coedited a monthly column with Michael Casey in *Library Journal* for over two years. He has written articles that have appeared in *Public Libraries, Library Journal, American Libraries, Computers in Libraries, Library Media Connection, OCLC's NextSpace,* and ALA's *TechSource* blog. He serves on the editorial board of both *Reference and Users Services Quarterly* and *Internet Reference Services Quarterly.*

Perhaps the most well read of Michael's professional writing endeavors is his weblog, *Tame the Web,* also known as *TTW* (http://tametheweb.com). Launched in 2003, the blog addresses issues involving libraries, technology, and people, "and the fascinating intersection between all three." Frequent items of discussion on the blog include using technology to further a library's mission, how technology is used in learning, and what innovative librarians are doing to explore the realm of technology. "Sadly," says Michael, "my blog doesn't count for tenure, but the opportunities it has brought to me have certainly added to my portfolio."

A typical midweek workday for Michael begins with a view of the sunrise while drinking a cup of tea. "I go to bed early these days because there is tea waiting in the morning and I really enjoy watching the sun come up," he says. After posting to *TTW,* catching up on e-mail, and looking over his "to-do list," he heads to campus. "I usually have late morning office hours in order to be available for the daytime or full-time students, but usually I don't see anyone in person," he says. "These days, most of our students are so busy—working full-time and balancing life and school—that a phone call or e-mail is easier. E-mails from students or a Facebook question might come in. I have on occasion Skyped with a student, or iChatted if we both have Macs." Michael also spends his morning office hours checking citation formats for articles in progress or finishing a longer blog post. Lunch hour is either spent with colleagues or spent looking over materials for evening classes he teaches. "If it's toward the end of the semester, I might also be grading research papers or shorter responses to various articles. I look for critical thinking, flow of argument, and error-free writing. We have to be able to communicate effectively in writing in our profession. Grading, in general, puts me through the paces because I so want students to do well. I've really grown in that aspect these past few semesters. It's hard to grade down, but I hope it ultimately helps the student grow."

Some Wednesday afternoons, Michael attends Faculty Council meetings. As chair of the GSLIS IT Committee, he shares meeting minutes with university faculty. "The funny thing is, I was very quiet in early meetings my first and second year teaching," he says. "I felt it was better to get the lay of the land before talking too much. I'm not so quiet anymore. Recently, I reported on our committee's ongoing work with new technologies for teaching such as AdobeConnect. Other reports are shared and there is general discussion—and some laugh-out-loud moments, too!" After Faculty Council, Michael heads into downtown Chicago where he teaches courses in off-site locations such as the Chicago Public Library. "This semester I'm teaching LIS701, Introduction to Library and Information Science, in the Chicago Public Library's Staff Development Office Training Room. I have office hours for the downtown students from 4 to 5 p.m. at Panera Bread on State Street. In class, we discuss the week's articles, I lecture a bit, and then the students break out into discussion groups. Last night, for example, we spent two hours on collection development. I absolutely love this module and enjoy sharing some of my stories of past public library experiences." After class, he is done for the day and finally heads home.

"The most unique things about the job for me are the scheduling and the morphing nature of LIS programs in general," Michael says. "It's always different. I might teach one night a week or two nights or have weekend classes, all while also teaching online or in the blended format. Because I relocated part-time to Illinois with my main residence in Indiana, I've done a lot of driving back and forth but have also participated in meetings, taught, had advising appointments, and created course content from my home office in Mishawaka, Indiana. The nature of LIS programs is changing: more online, more scheduling opportunities to make it easier for the full-time worker to get the degree. This means the nature of professors' work changes as well. I gladly give up three weekends to teach an intensive course because it helps the students and frees up time for me during the week for research and writing. I am also on the road a few times a semester, doing talks for libraries, consortia, and library associations. The flexible nature of the work affords this and makes it easier to do a talk somewhere and get back for class."

Technology has played a large role throughout Michael's education and career. He has a B.A. in telecommunications, with a minor in film studies/comparative literature, from Indiana University. "After my undergrad, I was a little aimless; working at the local TV station no longer seemed to fit and I found myself working in a music/video store. I loved helping people find what they were looking for but never enjoyed the profit motives and the hours," he says. When he took a job as assistant head of audiovisual services at the St. Joseph County Public Library (SJCPL) in South Bend, Indiana, he realized he was still working in customer service—but without the dollar signs! While there, Michael got his first taste of technology training: six computers in his department were for public use, and he assisted users with word processing, scanning, and page layout. Michael moved on to a position in Reference Services, where he experienced "the true big picture of library service."

Michael enrolled in Indiana University's M.L.I.S. program while continuing to work at SJCPL. During that time, in 1994, SJCPL became the first public library in the United States to offer Internet access and to mount a web page. "From then on, my focus in reference shifted toward online services, searching, and presenting information electronically," he says. "We developed a training program for staff on how to use the Internet resources we offered, how to answer questions with various Gopher and Web sites, and how to answer library users' questions. Later, we began to offer 'Beginning Internet' classes for the public, and a year later we were hosting 100–125 people in our large community room for each class. I loved this and still do: presenting something so cool as the Web to groups of curious people."

After completing his master's degree, he took a job at SJCPL as staff technology trainer, where he was responsible for educating the entire library staff on current and emerging technologies and networked resources. He was later named the head of the Networked Resources Development and Training Department. He continued in that position until 2004, when he decided to pursue a Ph.D. in order to become a library school professor. He was awarded an IMLS (Institute of Museum and Library Services) fellowship to attend a Ph.D. program at the University of North Texas, where he conducted research on social software and blogging and completed a dissertation entitled "Modeling the Role of Blogging in Librarianship." "Pursuing the Ph.D. was one of the best things that ever happened to me," he says. "With my mentor and advisor Dr. Brian O'Connor, we created a plan of study where I could follow my interests and learn all I could about research design as well as online communities and social interaction online. This led to my research concerning librarian bloggers." In 2006 he was hired into his current position at Dominican University.

Michael continues to be an expert on technology in libraries, and is often invited to give presentations—sometimes keynote addresses—at professional meetings. He has spoken about technology, innovation, and libraries to audiences in over twenty five states and in four countries, including a recent speaking tour in Australia. For example, he recently presented "Creative Collaboration and Immersive Engagement: The Hyperlinked Campus" at the EDUCAUSE Learning Initiative Annual Meeting in Austin, Texas. He presented preliminary results from his Australian research project— "Measuring the Value and Effect of Learning 2.0 Programs in Public Libraries"—at the Public Library Association annual meeting in Portland, Oregon. He delivered several presentations at a conference for librarians, social media professionals, and embassy employees in Germany, and he gave a Dean's and Director's Lecture at the School of Library and Information Science at the University of South Carolina.

To keep up with technology, Michael monitors technology and trend blogs, reads publications such as *Wired* and *Fast Company,* and "anything else that points to changes in how society consumes information." "I seek out learning opportunities as much as I can," he says. "I attend a lot of conferences all over the world, usually to speak but also to listen. I am especially excited about conferences I've attended in the UK and Holland, where international librarians come together to share and exchange ideas." He is a member of the American Library Association and the Association for Library and Information Science Education. In 2005 he was named a "Mover and Shaker" by *Library Journal.*

Michael loves to talk to people who are interested in pursuing their Ph.D. in order to be able to teach in LIS programs. "I encourage them to follow that interest, investigate the opportunities, and if it seems like a good fit, to jump in," he says. "I'd especially encourage those who are interested in emerging issues in our field, such as digital collections and the organization of information on a global scale." He also stresses the importance of learning from colleagues even after securing a position as an LIS professor. "My doctorate program did not include 'how to manage a classroom' or 'how to handle student problems,'" he says. "Those things you pick up as you go along. I was lucky in my first year at Dominican because I had a wonderful faculty mentor, Dr. Kate Marek, who guided me and was always available for advice."

In looking to the future, Michael encourages librarians to become trend-spotters. "If we scan the horizon," he says, "we're trend-spotting for the future. I am so inspired by the librarians who try new things, who look outside the field and bring things back. If we become trend-spotters, we have a good chance of creating the 'next big thing.' We might simply ponder, for example, what the popularity of a certain technology might do to library service. Or what bigger trends will mean to libraries in the next 10–20 years. I watch Apple, Starbucks, and Amazon right now among many others. Couldn't we have a genius bar in our libraries (I know the library in Delft does!)? Couldn't we tap into marketing the 'third place' the way Starbucks does so well? And isn't there a place for the new concepts Borders will be offering: digital downloads, media creation, etc.? If we make sure to be curious about the world, it makes all of the above super easy."

This ties in closely with Michael's philosophy of teaching. "Libraries and librarians are faced with a technological and societal wave of change that is ever increasing as we move farther into the twenty-first century," he says. "Preparing new graduates to deal with constant change, use current and emerging technology tools to further the mission of their institutions, and meet the needs of communities of library users, while never losing sight of our foundational values and principles, is of utmost importance to me as an LIS educator. If my students leave my classes as curious librarians ready to figure out the 'next big thing' and make it work in their libraries," he concludes, "then I am doing my job."

Michael would like to share his "Five Hopes for the New Year," a reflection on librarianship in past years and on what the future will bring to our profession. "I get very excited at the power and promise of what we're doing: innovative services, new buildings, and harnessing new technologies to extend our services in surprising ways," he says. "With that in mind, I offer for this shiny new year a few simple hopes: (1) that we tell our story well; (2) that we guide our users into the digital landscape; (3) that we make cost-effective decisions; (4) that we open our doors to everyone; and (5) that we encourage the heart."

Michael recommends the following websites:

- http://tametheweb.com/the-hyperlinked-library/ (Michael's vision of the twenty-first-century library, called the "Hyperlinked Library")
- www.librarybeat.org/longshots/play/100/ ("Library Beat" podcast on Michael and his "Hyperlinked Library" vision)
- www.collegeonline.org/library/librarians-online/michael-stephens/ ("College Online's" interview of Michael)

JEANNINE M. BROWN

Library Media Specialist, Lakeland Elementary Library, Lakeland, Tennessee

"Librarians as educators need to provide a nurturing environment that fosters a love of reading in children and encourages them to become successful lifelong learners."

TRAINED AS a teacher with a B.S. in education and a master's in reading from the University of Memphis, Jeannine Brown taught in elementary and preschools for twenty-five years. Her love of books and reading led her to return to college to add library certification to her teaching certificate. She took thirty semester hours in library instruction and computer technology at the University of Memphis and now boasts the "Master's +45" certification. "My years as a librarian have been the most enjoyable of my teaching career," Jeannine says. "On the flip side, I think my experience as a classroom teacher has helped me to be a better librarian."

As the library media specialist at Lakeland Elementary School in Lakeland, Tennessee, Jeannine's work routine varies daily. "When I was in library school, my professor joked that everyone thinks all librarians do is sit in the library and eat bonbons all day," she says. Her list of responsibilities is more than enough to dispel that particular misconception. She begins each morning with carpool duty followed by a 35-minute period of open circulation, during which students may check out or return books. After that, her teaching schedule begins. She teaches library instruction classes back-to-back, with only a 5-minute break in between. She has 30 minutes for lunch and an hour in the afternoons for library management, cataloging books, pulling materials for teachers, and other last-minute duties that arise. At the end of the day, after another short open circulation period, she backs up the automated system and stays for another half hour to "wrap things up." "It makes for a busy day," she says, "but the days never drag by. In my eight years as a librarian, I can count on one hand the number of days I haven't been excited about going to school."

During her teaching sessions, Jeannine focuses on helping children to become independent library users. "It is so exciting to see the children look up books in the catalog, write down a call number, and actually find the book on the shelf without asking for help!" she says. She loves sharing books with children and reading to them, and feels a sense of accomplishment when she helps a child connect with a book.

In addition to her role as a librarian with a full teaching load, Jeannine is assigned various other duties. She is the school's technology assets manager, she is a member of the Certified Emergency Response Team, she is the Accelerated Reader administrator, and she was recently assigned the task of overseeing the schoolwide inventory of assets from AV equipment to computers to kitchen equipment and "everything in between." Fortunately, she has one assistant in the library to help alleviate some of the burden.

As do most school library media specialists, Jeannine must deal with constant challenges. Her school has a student population of over a thousand, and she finds it difficult to adequately serve them. Since she sees each class only once every other week, it is challenging to keep continuity in the lessons. Relationships with teachers can be tricky as well, especially when some view the librarian as a babysitter rather than a partner in education. "I don't approve of the teacher who daily checks out a video to show her class, but I am not the video police," she says. "Then there is the teacher who checks out fifty books to keep in her classroom and then can't keep up with them. Or the one that wants to check out the encyclopedia set for a few days and then keeps it indefinitely. You just have to smile and keep your mouth shut."

Jeannine maintains that school librarians must be flexible. Often she has her schedule carefully planned for the day, only to have a teacher drop off her class and say, "The students need a book for a realistic fiction book report, at least 100 pages in length, and it has to be an Accelerated Reader book." In such a situation, she has two choices: either continue with her lesson plans and then give twenty-five mini-lessons on realistic fiction books to each of the students, or ditch the lesson and do one group lesson off the top of her head about realistic fiction. "This will happen," she says, "despite the fact that you ask teachers to give you a 'heads-up.'"

Technology plays a large role in Jeannine's job. She maintains the automated circulation system, creates PowerPoint presentations, does podcasts of books, communicates via e-mail, and maintains the library website that is used by teachers, students, and parents. In addition, she is familiar with the various websites and databases for use by students working on homework or research projects. She also teaches an Internet safety curriculum as dictated by the school district. "The Internet is rapidly changing the way students access information," she remarks. "Librarians must be proactive to keep pace with those changes." She feels that school librarians in particular have evolved into information specialists due to the necessity of sifting through the information students encounter on the Internet. She says, "It is our responsibility to teach students how to evaluate and use all this electronic information. At the same time, we have to help them understand that much of the same information can be acquired through print materials. We have many students who have never seen or used a print encyclopedia. They think Wikipedia is an authoritative information source." She does stress that it is important for school librarians to be open to learning about the new ways students access information.

She believes that librarians must become lifelong learners themselves. "You're either green and growing or rotting in the pot," she says. Librarians must be proactive to keep pace with changing technology. Jeannine takes technology classes throughout the school year, seeks out networks that can help her keep current, attends conferences, and maintains memberships in professional organizations. In the past, she has been a member of the International Reading Association, American Library Association, American Association of School Librarians, and the Tennessee Association of School Librarians. In 2007 she was the recipient of the Tennessee Association of School Librarians' Innovative Library Media Program Award.

To those interested in becoming school library media specialists, Jeannine says, "Being a librarian can be a lonely job, especially if you are the only one in your school. It is important to create your own network with other librarians in your area and beyond. You'll then have people you can turn to for help and support. I wouldn't have survived my first year without the help of the librarians I connected with in my university library classes."

When Jeannine first began her career, a mentor said to her, "Being a librarian is like eating an elephant. You do it one spoonful at a time." In time, she came to realize what this meant. "Many times the tasks I have to do as a librarian seem overwhelming," she explains, "but I try to break the tasks down into 'spoonfuls' that I can handle one at a time."

Jeannine suggests the following websites:

- http://teacherlibrarian.ning.com (a teacher/librarian social network; a great source of information on current technologies)
- http://lakelandes.scsk12.org/~brownj/ (her own Lakeland Library website)
- www.storylineonline.net/index2.html (features streaming video of actors reading picture books)

SCOTT WALTER

Associate University Librarian for Services, Associate Dean of Libraries,
Professor of Library Administration and Library and Information Science,
University of Illinois at Urbana-Champaign, Urbana, Illinois

*"I see the educational role as one of the core
professional responsibilities of the librarian."*

SCOTT WALTER is a big believer in training librarians to be educators. "In order to maintain our relevance at a time when traditional information needs are being met outside of the context of the physical library," he says, "it becomes essential for us to prepare librarians to view the teaching role as central to their professional identity. It is critical for the librarian to effectively articulate his or her educational role as related to the needs of the user community. Librarians must have the professional skills necessary to identify learning goals for users, design instruction aimed at helping users achieve those goals, deliver that instruction effectively, and assess the impact of the instruction on student learning."

In keeping with his philosophy on librarians as educators, one of Scott's primary responsibilities at the University of Illinois (UI) at Urbana-Champaign is to ensure that the librarians have the support they need to have success in their teaching roles. "I work with our instruction coordinator and our User Education Committee to meet the teaching needs of our librarians," he says. "This may involve providing support for professional development activities—both local and national—or obtaining resources such as those that provided for the construction of our new instruction lab. My role is also to foster connections between library instructional initiatives and campus instructional initiatives in areas such as undergraduate research. I also help foster connections between traditional information literacy instruction efforts and emergent teaching efforts, as in the field of scholarly communications education."

Scott says that from the teaching perspective, his greatest challenge continues to be fostering creativity and commitment among librarians regarding their teaching role and promoting a greater understanding of that role among the classroom faculty. "I've written about the fact that our profession includes many people who were brought into librarianship before the teaching role was recognized as a core professional responsibility of all librarians," he says. "While we always have innovators blazing the way in establishing effective instructional partnerships between librarians and others, there is an ongoing effort needed to have this work broadly recognized as essential to the librarian role on campus, both inside and outside the library."

In his role as associate librarian for services, Scott ensures that library service programs are aligned with campus initiatives. "I try to foster a common vision of service programs across the library," he says. "I work to identify opportunities for collaboration with campus colleagues and to facilitate the success of our library faculty and staff."

In addition to serving as associate dean of libraries, Scott holds a faculty appointment as professor of library administration and library and information science. He has taught several graduate-level courses, including "Reference and Information Services" and "Libraries, Information, and Society," at both the UI Graduate School of Library and Information Science and the San José State University School of Library and Information Science. He also holds an affiliate appointment in the College of Education's Higher Education Program.

Scott's work is dependent upon technology in significant ways. "The primary way in which technology affects my work is in the need to ensure that librarians have access to technology-enhanced teaching spaces and to relevant software applications," he says. "I must also ensure that library instructional efforts align with broader campus efforts around technology-enhanced teaching. This may involve placing librarians on campus committees looking at topics such as e-portfolios or learning object repositories, or on campus educational technology groups such as those looking at the use of online course environments. It may involve placing librarians on campus groups looking at emergent instructional needs not currently well supported at the campus level—copyright education, education in the use of digital content (text, data, images), etc."

Scott has written several research articles in peer-reviewed journals related to librarians as teachers and educators. He makes a point of stressing certain key skills needed for librarians to be successful teachers. These are (1) pedagogical skills (those related directly to classroom teaching); (2) instructional design skills (those related both to developing instruction and to assessing the impact of instruction on student learning); and (3) "border-crossing" skills (awareness of instructional initiatives and issues in the broader higher education environment, and the ability to translate learning objectives to the members of the scholarly community with which one is hoping to collaborate).

Scott has a B.S. in Russian and linguistics and an M.A. in Russian area studies, both from Georgetown University. He received an M.A. in education from American University and was in the process of earning a Ph.D. at Indiana University when he "discovered" library school. He completed his M.L.S. at Indiana and later received an M.S. in history and philosophy of education from the same institution. Finally, he earned his Ph.D. in higher education administration from Washington State University.

"I became interested in librarianship while working on my Ph.D. at Indiana," Scott explains. "As a doctoral student, I received significant experience in research and teaching, but was not encouraged by the prospects for work in my field. I had worked as a library staff member at American University and the Urban Institute in the early 1990s, and when a classmate in my doctoral program completed his M.L.S. and went off to what seemed like a satisfying career, I decided to look at librarianship more closely. I entered the LIS program thinking that the closest connection with my previous plans would be in research and in my background with rare books and special collections (I had trained as a historian), but I quickly found that the best connection was with the aspect of librarianship that I knew nothing about—teaching."

While he did not take formal courses related to his work as a teacher, Scott did complete an internship in which the focus was developing an instructional program. He also worked in the Undergraduate Library at Indiana. "Both are examples of the critical role played in the pre-service education of instruction librarians by 'field' experiences," he says. "The LIS curriculum, as a whole, continues to neglect this critical aspect of librarianship (except for the pre-service school librarians). The role of the academic library as a provider of field experiences that complement the pre-service education provided in the LIS classroom cannot be overestimated."

Scott is a member of the American Library Association, the Association for Library and Information Science Education, the Association for Library Collections and Technical Services, the Association of College and Research Libraries, the Illinois Library Association, the Library Leadership and Management Association, the California Teachers Association, and other professional organizations. "Participation in professional and scholarly associations is critical," he says, "especially those where one can make a connection with like-minded colleagues outside libraries." He attends continuing education programs and professional conferences.

To those interested in teaching within the field of librarianship, Scott says, "Take every opportunity to learn broadly about college teaching, faculty development programs, and campus instructional initiatives. These opportunities not only help you to develop as a professional, but provide you with the broader context for your work necessary for success in the twenty-first century (where a focus on 'library instruction' and even 'instruction in the library' will lead to a truncated vision of your role and the role of the library on campus). It is through the role of the library representative to campus discussions that one finds the opportunities for collaboration that have proven so right over the past decade, including collaboration with writing centers, teaching centers, student affairs programs, first-year experience, and undergraduate research initiatives.

"Being a librarian today means the same thing as it always has—we build collections for our users, we provide services they need to make use of those collections or to otherwise meet their information needs, we preserve our cultural heritage and ensure its ongoing accessibility, we contribute to local and national discussions on issues such as censorship, access to information, and the right to privacy and intellectual freedom," Scott says. "What has changed in recent years is the size of the playing field, the nature of the issues we are asked to address, and the ways in which the significance of information issues for all of us have reshaped the way in which our role on campus and in society is envisioned. Changes in technology have reshaped the way we create, use, reuse, and preserve information in every part of our society, and that has taken what was once the unique professional responsibility of the librarian or archivist and made it of interest to a much broader range of individuals. This has required us to undertake a fundamental reconsideration of what comprise the core professional responsibilities of the librarian. The educational role of the librarian is one of those core responsibilities—possibly the most important one."

Scott recommends the following websites:

- https://netfiles.uiuc.edu/swalter/www/instructional_improvement.html (Scott's "Instructional Improvement in Academic Libraries" web page)
- http://writingcenters.org (International Writing Centers Association)
- http://naspa.org (NASPA: Students Affairs Administrators in Higher Education)
- www.sc.edu/fye/ (National Resource Center for the First Year Experience and Students in Transition)
- www.cur.org (Council on Undergraduate Research)
- www.teachingprofessor.com (The Teaching Professor)
- http://information-literacy.blogspot.com (*Information Literacy* weblog)
- www.comminfolit.org/index.php/cil/ (*Communications in Information Literacy*)

BRIAN MATHEWS

User Experience Librarian, Library and Information Center,
Georgia Institute of Technology, Atlanta, Georgia

*"We take an empathic approach to our users; that is, we consider the
needs of the users and then try to build ways to meet those needs."*

BRIAN MATHEW'S job is unique. As user experience librarian at Georgia Tech's Library and Information Center, it is his responsibility to "make the library better." "It goes far beyond mere satisfaction or even comprehension of library services," he explains, "but something that is more visceral. I really try to push an empathic approach—that is, we consider the needs of users and then try to build a way to provide a solution—rather than the typical approach in which libraries try to promote their wares.

"Not many libraries think about the 'experience' of the library user—the totality, the emotional connection that users have with our building, resources, and services," Brian says. This is what makes his job unique. "My role involves assessment and marketing and is very experimental." His primary clientele are the undergraduate students of Georgia Tech, followed by the graduate students and the faculty. His secondary patrons are the library staff; he works across departments on promotional and assessment needs.

"I spend a lot of time talking with students to find out where they have problems or frustrations—with the library or beyond," Brian says. "What are the tough classes? What are the tough assignments? What do they spend time doing? What are the roadblocks, stumbling blocks, uncertainties? Once you uncover that information, you have a surefire way to gain success. I try to position the library to address special needs—academic, social, cultural, leisure. In short, instead of a message that goes like this: 'We have these great databases; let me tell you all about them,' I am much more interested in a conversation like this: 'Tell me about your assignments; hmmmm, interesting, maybe I can help you.'

"The most challenging aspect of my job is getting 'buy-in.' I feel I am always selling ideas, always selling needs, always trying to bring people together," Brian says. "I have learned that I need to be more holistic, and that's a challenge for me. Our atmosphere is very fragmented; you have lots of people working on different things, so it's challenging to try to find out what's going on and how I might be able to help or get involved."

There is no set schedule for Brian's workdays. "Each day is different," he says. "My job is very project-oriented. I try to look at things two weeks at a time. For example, right now I'm working with staff to develop a library logo, a visual identity. Last week I spent a good chunk of time prepping for two upcoming presentations. The week before that we hosted a furniture showcase for students to test out chairs and tables that we will purchase for our upcoming renovation.

"It's hard to describe day-to-day activities," he continues. "I'd say I spend about two hours a day writing e-mails. Another hour reading—books, maybe other people's e-mail, reports, the school newspaper, campus documents, blogs, etc. I spend another hour walking around the library and campus—absorbing what's going on, meeting and chatting with people. I have a goal to meet two new students a week, which I feed into a database for potential library programming partners or who can provide feedback when needed. Probably two hours a day are filled with meetings. And the rest of the time varies—working on projects, the reference desk, instruction, web work; it just depends. A lot of times there is a pressing project that I focus a great deal of time on and then that goes away and I play catch-up with other duties. There is a definite ebb and flow."

Brian makes use of technology for social communication. "I use my iPhone all the time," he says. "I use Facebook to 'talk' with students. I use AOL IM (instant messaging) to talk with library staff." He maintains a personal blog called *The Ubiquitous Librarian* in which he shares information and thoughts on "user-sensitive librarianship." He also contributes to a blog called *Designing Better Libraries: Exploring the Application of Design, Innovation, and New Media to Create Better Libraries and User Experiences.* These blogs chronicle his experiments and ideas regarding his work.

To keep up with trends, Brian reads *Wired, Fast Company, Ad Age,* and the *Chronicle of Higher Education.* "I learn about technology from my students," he says. "Twitter and Facebook aid that process. I also hear about things from other librarians—mostly via Twitter, and sometimes through blogs or articles. I do attend conferences, but most of the stuff I hear at conferences is a year behind the curve." He is a member of the American Library Association, the Association of College and Research Libraries, and the Library Leadership and Management Association.

Typical of those in the field, Brian did not start out wanting to become a librarian. In fact, he wanted to be a journalist. "All during high school I wrote articles and planned a career in the newspaper field," he says. "I think that gave me an edge over many of my peers in terms of writing, research, and critical thinking because newspaper activities forced me to produce regular articles. In college I learned that I wrote too slowly and only liked writing about things I was passionate about. Hence, I would not have made a good journalist."

Brian earned a double B.A. in English and history from the University of Central Florida (UCF). While at UCF, he worked as a student assistant in the library, checking in and reshelving books. When he graduated, the lure of the library kept hold of him, and he took a full-time job as a paraprofessional in circulation, where he supervised ten student assistants. "At the time I was considering graduate school and was leaning toward history, but found librarianship to be enticing," he says. "It would still allow me to have an academic career, to write and present, and be surrounded by scholarly enterprise. So it seemed like a good fit. I earned my M.L.S. from the University of South Florida in 2001. My first professional job was at George Washington University, where I was a reference and instruction librarian. I dabbled in many areas there, particularly assessment and web development. After three years, I left Washington, D.C., for Atlanta and took a job at Georgia Tech. I was an information services librarian, basically reference and instruction, and served the School of Mechanical Engineering and the College of Computing. I was also the coordinator of distance learning services. My job evolved and I emerged outside of reference into leading what is now called the User Experience Unit."

Brian is the author of *Marketing Today's Academic Library: A Bold New Approach to Communicating with Students* (ALA Editions, 2009). He has written book chapters on social networking and on alternatives to traditional reference work. He has also authored several peer-reviewed journal articles and has given numerous presentations on marketing the library and methods of interacting with library patrons.

According to Brian, skills that are important for librarians working in positions similar to his include curiosity, storytelling, analytical thinking, brainstorming, meeting facilitation, writing and presenting, small-talk skills, salesmanship, design, and creativity. "I would recommend that librarians find their own paths," he says. "I borrow heavily from other disciplines—marketing, anthropology, industrial design. I would advise others to study methods from other professions and find logical ways to integrate them into their library. I would also urge them to study their patrons. What works for me at Georgia Tech might not work in all libraries. We have a very specific clientele here. A big problem in librarianship is that everyone copies each other—there is a lack of originality in the big picture. So I would urge people to think differently.

"I was in college when the Web was blooming," Brian says. "What I saw was librarians (or library vendors) adopting new technologies but keeping the same work processes. Today, we should have great databases and catalogs, like Amazon or iTunes, but instead we have second-rate interfaces. I see the same approach filtering into social software. Librarians raced to get Facebook profiles and Second Life reference desks, expecting to do more of the same, just in a different place, rather than learning the culture of web tools or virtual environments and creating something new—a new service or new channel/method of interacting. I think that is a flaw in our profession. We are quick to jump on 'hot trends' but don't use them fully. We are good at adopting but bad at adapting.

"I think we're going to continue to see a big divide in the profession as more and more technology plays a role," Brian concludes. "There will be a greater need for people to program metalib, the catalog, and web design. We'll still need people to help, but there will be a great advantage to people who can program. We'll still need subject experts, but I see greater influence and need for people with computer skills. They will be in greater demand. Looking to the future: if access is the key, then it will be the people granting access that really shape the library experience."

For more information about Brian and his interests, visit:

- http://theubiquitouslibrarian.typepad.com (*The Ubiquitous Librarian,* Brian's blog)
- http://dbl.lishost.org/blog/ (*Designing Better Libraries*)

DARREN G. POLEY

Outreach Librarian, Programming Team Leader, Falvey Memorial Library, Villanova University, Villanova, Pennsylvania

"Every community has a story; some of it lost, some of it hidden, and some of it needing to be better known. The outreach librarian can either aid others in the discovery of the story or work to contribute to its unfolding."

DARREN POLEY is an academic librarian whose job falls outside the traditional and strict "lines of demarcation" that characterized the profession for decades. Whereas in the past, academic librarians were classified as either "public services" (with reference at the top) or "technical services" (to include cataloging, acquisitions, serials, and systems), people like Darren are now seen as examples of forward-thinking library professionals who thrive by tearing down barriers to collaboration. This is a very complex way of saying that as environments change, librarians like Darren are able to transform themselves in order to remain relevant.

What exactly does it mean to be an "outreach librarian" in an academic library? In his position at Villanova University (VU), a private Catholic institution in Pennsylvania, Darren's responsibilities are varied. He is in charge of cultural and intellectual programming in the library, including public events and displays. He also spearheads efforts by the library to be more visibly involved in campus life. "This can be either participation with things already going on," he explains, "or building bridges to get a project going that will partner the library with other entities. I have a team of about ten people who dedicate various fractions of time to programming and outreach work. I have organized the team so individual members have discrete areas of responsibility based on their own talents, interests, and overall work schedule.

"My position grew over time along with the redevelopment of the human organization for the library," Darren says. He started off at VU as a reference/catalog librarian at the rank of librarian I. He soon earned a promotion to the rank of library professional II. Several years later, he moved to a newly created position entitled coordinator of programming and outreach, which then changed to his current title of outreach librarian and programming team leader. He has since earned the rank of librarian III.

"When I first started there it was important to be available to answer questions, and if you were ambitious you took on special projects," Darren says. "Now I handle mostly special projects while still doing traditional collection development and research support activities. Although most of my reference interviews come from referrals or appointments, instruction and collection building stem from liaison work in my subject specialty. In one way I have become less of a generalist when it comes to research assistance and the library collections. On the other hand, I have had to become more widely versed in a bunch of skills that draw upon my previous training or acuity."

In his outreach mode, Darren spends a lot of time in meetings. "Consulting with team members, faculty, and students is a daily need," he says. "After all, I'm supposed to reach out to people and that translates into meetings, whether they are one-on-one appointments, committees I am on, or groups I have gathered for a purpose." Since he is often out of the office, he relies heavily on technology to keep him available and connected. "I was one of the early adopters of having a laptop rather than a desk-bound PC," he says. "This way I could make presentations, do instruction, stay on top of e-mail anywhere, and basically carry around my office with me. The difficulty with a job like mine is that everyone expects you everywhere all the time. When my boss and I talk about being pulled in so many directions, which I credit to instant communication and information portability, he says perhaps that is the life of a twenty-first-century librarian. At home I am pretty low-tech, but at work I take advantage of the 'toys' to make communication more convenient."

Darren starts his workday at 7 a.m. when his BlackBerry turns on. He commutes to and from work by train and uses that travel time to clean up e-mail correspondence before even arriving at the office. He also makes lists of things requiring his attention, writes notes to himself, and sends information to team members. "I can do all this on the BlackBerry before I get 'sidetracked' by all the things waiting in the workplace for me to tackle," he says. "Having the BlackBerry has revolutionized my ability to do work, to be at work anywhere, and be available even when I am out of the office.

"My job is primarily high touch rather than high tech, except in the use of methods for quick and reliable communication, which is essential," Darren continues. "The biggest part of my job is the need to think about many different things simultaneously. Because you can only actively think about one thing at a time, multitasking for me means being organized. You constantly have to juggle many demands and various ideas that are floating out there. If you don't get yourself organized—and this is where technology is important—you will not be able to stay on top of things. Managing all the different needs and priorities that involve human and other resources is the main thing I do while at the same time producing results from collaborative efforts on many different projects."

The library's primary patrons are the students, faculty, and staff of the university. However, on a day-to-day basis, Darren works more with faculty and administrators of the university. He also works with clerics and other ecclesiastics, as well as library directors, archivists, and librarians from other institutions. "I deal with a highly educated group overall," he says. "It is an interesting mix of formality and informality. This is a rather 'buttoned-down campus' compared with many universities today."

One of Darren's biggest tasks as outreach librarian is to serve as a catalyst for technological change. "I don't mind being the bridge between techies and librarians," he says. "This requires the skill of listening, learning, and the willingness to be vulnerable about your own shortcomings. One good example of this theory in action is a project I spearheaded: the negotiation of a digital partnership between the library and the oldest Catholic historical society in the United States. The society has an incomparable collection of rare printed materials that is basically in uncataloged storage. My library wanted to make them widely available by scanning them and making the digital files freely available to scholars. We were successful in this negotiation. This is a good example of what it means to build bridges as a community liaison that stemmed from a combination of several of my interests and responsibilities."

Darren recounts that his unique job was at first treated with disdain by his professional colleagues. People were not initially receptive to the new library director's goal of "tearing down old silos of responsibility" and transforming the work environment. "I knew I had to change with the environment and find my niche in the organization, so I began to get involved with some dramatic transformations. I worked on the reinvigoration of the library liaison system, I got involved in strategic planning processes, and I was involved in making improvements and renovations to the library facility. I was direct and open with my boss as to ideas I had concerning projects and innovations. All of this advanced me on a path that set me apart from my fellow librarians as a risk taker. It is risky being a gadfly, and ambition is not always highly prized among librarians, particularly those set in their ways.

"I got a lot of support, though, from my boss," he continues, "because I produced results and brought positive change that advanced the library in its mission. I am a pretty traditional guy. I don't look for change just to be rebellious or cool. Nevertheless, in this case it made me a lightning rod for the feelings about the changes happening in the profession and in our workplace. As one librarian who was younger and newer put it, 'The reference librarian position has always been the coveted plum job in the library, and you have betrayed all that for something that is potentially a lot more work.' As my boss put it when we decided to officially change my role in the library midstream, during the academic and fiscal years, 'You are now officially the chief neck sticker-outer.' This was when I became the coordinator of programming and outreach."

For Darren, the change from doing a little bit of programming and outreach to being the sole person in charge was "heady, crazy, and a true professional challenge." In his previous positions, he had a period of training. In this he was on his own. "This was breaking new ground for me personally as well as professionally," he says. "The workload quickly became an overwhelming set of demanding, time-sensitive, and highly visible responsibilities. I never wanted to let an opportunity or a good idea go by without attempting to make it happen. I had the freedom to experiment and basically try to do great things. I quickly saw my limits, but success was the engine that drove me to want to get more involved and to do more.

"Ultimately the reorganization of the entire library caught up to me and I was made one of several team leaders in the library," Darren continues. "Every job was now blended in a matrixed organization. How my unique role functions in relationship to the academic integration team, or the communication and publications team, for example, is still evolving. I do serve some on the digital library team and on a liaison team, and this diversity can be fragmenting, but also gives a healthy outlet to my other interests that are not included in my primary role. The largest balancing act on my part is really between the management of a team that I hope to inspire to produce great things while still achieving positive results in my own work."

Darren says that because technology is for everyone, young and old, it is "transformative" and continues to transform the ways people do things. It is therefore important to stay connected with trends in the profession. "Being connected to professional colleagues is also important," he says. "You must have a commitment to your own professional development. No one will pay you for just being the smartest person in the room. Working with smart people, and this includes involvement in professional associations, is key." He is a member of the American Library Association, the Association of College and Research Libraries, and the Catholic Library Association.

Darren has a B.A. in classical studies and political science and an M.A. in religion. While looking for work after grad school, he found that the library job ads in the *Chronicle of Higher Education* sounded more appealing than the teaching and administrative jobs. "What I also realized was that I had always worked in libraries as a student, ever since junior high," he says. "I loved libraries. I always had. I am excited by books, the gathered collections of human knowledge, and the figuring out of questions that need to be answered for reasons of either curiosity or erudition. Then there was the time when I was pulling an all-nighter in college with a fellow undergrad who told me, 'You should be a librarian. You are a wealth of useless information.' My fate was sealed." Darren did some research on library schools and enrolled at the School of Information Science and Technology at Drexel University. Upon completion of his M.S. in information science and technology, he took a position as public services librarian at the Lutheran Theological Seminary in Philadelphia, where he had been working as a technical services assistant. He also began working part-time as a reference librarian at Villanova University. A few years later he began working full-time at Falvey Memorial Library and has been there ever since.

Darren's advice to those interested in librarianship is to hone organizational skills and work on creating methods for managing details. "Librarians are not trained managers," he says. "But being a librarian today means being a manager—a manager of resources, needs, and demands. You need to be friendly with everyone, not really friends with anyone. What I mean is that as a manager you have to often make tough decisions, deal with difficult situations, and you need to take dispassionate and decisive action. At the same time you cannot run all over people or they will stop coming to you, and you will have a flat-out morale disaster on your hands. A librarian in my position must know how to juggle many projects, contacts, and many pieces of information simultaneously. The trick is not to be too bogged down in your work and to keep the optimism flowing. You need to be able to step back and take a fresh look at something, or at least keep an objective view.

"Garner as many skills as possible and groom your capacity to deal with people unless you want to work solely in IT," Darren continues. "The opportunities are greater if you have knowledge of languages—either computer code or a foreign language. Discover what you are good at and would like to do every day. Don't be a social worker, and don't be a social butterfly. Find out how you can contribute to the service mission of your employer and demonstrate the solutions you can offer to the challenges it faces. Get involved and keep learning. These are the keys to success.

"If you are interested in being a librarian involved with community interrelationships, know that every institution of education and communication is about telling stories," Darren concludes. "Every community has a story; some of it lost, some of it hidden, and some of it needing to be better known. The librarian as community liaison can aid in the discovery of the story or work to contribute to its unfolding. Librarians must constantly demonstrate the unique cultural contribution libraries make. Some things exist just to be enabling, and in the process, ennobling. This is what I think a librarian who is a community liaison does—they enable others either to find the more in-depth information they need, or to allow a library to be one of those cultural institutions that enriches the community it serves."

BRIGID CAHALAN

Older Adults Services Specialist, New York Public Library, New York, New York

"Librarians are the renaissance people of our day. We are the bridge between the past and the future and the ones who welcome the future while cherishing the past."

BRIGID CAHALAN's philosophy on libraries and librarianship is simple. "We should be the place—whether virtual or physical—where everything is happening, and where everyone wants to get together to talk, discuss, think, dream, and have fun!" she says. As the older adults services specialist at the New York Public Library (NYPL), Brigid is deeply involved with community outreach. In particular, she is charged with reaching out to a particular target audience: active older adults, aged fifty and over, in New York City. "When the position was instituted," she says, "I was asked to be sure to keep in mind one important category of older New Yorkers: those who had lived elsewhere and chose to come back to live in New York City after retirement."

Coordinating programs and services for her target population is exciting for Brigid. "I'm discovering there are a lot of librarians on our staff who are interested in programs and services for those 50+, and helping to channel those energies, while coordinating existing activities, is exciting," she says. "Capturing those 50+ (or 60+, 70+, or 80+) who have drifted away from the library since the demise of the card catalog and/or the birth of the big-box and online booksellers, and luring them back in, is definitely a challenge!"

When asked about her day-to-day routine, Brigid says there is no such thing. "I can't describe a daily routine," she explains, "beyond lots of e-mails, lots of web searching, lots of phone calls, lots of meetings. Every day is different depending on what projects I have in the works."

Being in the "50+" category herself, Brigid finds technology to be a challenge. "With the encouragement and support of colleagues, I (along with all the other employees who are 50+) am learning bit by bit," she says. "After the director suggested I start a professional blog—something I never could foresee myself doing—I did so, again with a *huge* amount of help. I find it has been both personally rewarding and a great way to get the word out about what you're learning and working on."

Brigid's first post on her blog (www.nypl.org/blog/2008/11/17/next-chapter-50 -library-blog/) reaches out to the "baby boomer" population. "Don't despair if you are a Boomer," the post reads. "The public library is with you every step of the way. Chances are you grew up going to your public library. But people have changed; they take advantage of the myriad options now available for getting information and spending leisure time. And libraries have changed; the passing of the card catalog since the 1980s has left some bereft of a lifelong friend. Libraries throughout the U.S. constantly retool to meet the needs of library users and, as librarians, we welcome the 50+ population, in its millions of manifestations, through our physical and virtual doors." She concludes the post with, "I'm starting this blog—my first—to share what we are doing at The New York Public Library to help enhance library services for the active older adult. Feel free to comment, suggest, nudge, blather, or whatever, as the spirit moves you." One particular comment in response to the blog post was poignant: "Good idea to keep in mind that a library should not only focus on those young of age, but also cater to those who have stayed young at heart."

Brigid keeps up with changes in the field by taking advantage of staff development opportunities offered by the library. "Some of these sessions are directly related to the job such as technology training, while others are of a more general life skills nature, for example, stress management and brain fitness. It's all good," she says. "I've also participated in some professional training on the national level; for instance, WebJunction's Spanish Language Outreach Training and Libraries for the Future's Lifelong Access Institute." She is a member of the New York Library Association, the American Library Association, and REFORMA (the National Association to

Promote Library and Information Services to Latinos and the Spanish-Speaking), and she attends conferences at the state, national, and international levels. "I often go to professional, library-related conferences, paying from my own pocket, because they are so useful to me," she says. "In particular, the New York Library Association has been hugely helpful since it has given me many ways to collaborate with colleagues in nearby systems and to meet so many people I wouldn't have had the opportunity to interact with otherwise. A bonus is that I would know virtually nothing about spectacular New York State if it weren't for the great conferences I've been to in all its diverse corners."

Brigid has a B.A. degree in Spanish from St. John's University in Queens, New York. After graduating, she had trouble finding full-time employment and worked as a temp and as a "semi-volunteer." "I look back fondly on those years today and am glad I didn't get a 'real' job for a few years," she says. "Since I wasn't tied down geographically I indulged my wanderlust and got a vague sense of what I might want, and *not* want, to do with the rest of my life. I visited a friend's mother who was head librarian in Ketchikan, Alaska, who convinced me that I might do well as a librarian. To my surprise, she considered that being particularly well organized was *not* an essential of a good librarian; far more important, in her experience as hirer and manager of many librarians over the years, were having a public service orientation and being interested in many things. I ended up promising her I'd apply for a job with the New York Public Library when I got back home to the East Coast. I did just that and got offered what was a dream job for a language major: working in the Foreign Language Library at the Donnell Library Center. I received the M.L.S. from Queens College of the City University of New York. And here at NYPL I remain, almost thirty years later."

When giving advice to those interested in public librarianship, particularly outreach, Brigid says that enthusiasm for the public library and librarianship is a must. Flexibility is also important, as well as a desire to keep learning, having an interest in what others are doing, and being eager to join forces to greater effect. She also recommends taking a class on public speaking and venturing outside of your comfort zone.

"The world moves so fast today, many of us feel we can't keep up; others are willing to die trying!" Brigid says. "Librarians are the renaissance people of our day: we are the bridge between the past and the future and the ones who welcome the future while cherishing the past. It reminds me of the old campfire song, 'Make new friends but keep the old; one is silver and the other gold.' Answers are cheap these days; if I'm not near a computer I just get them by calling an 800 number on my cell phone. But I want to know a source is trustworthy before I will trust it for something important. As information professionals we are more needed than ever to develop the skills to separate the wheat from the chaff. My career choice has forced me to become increasingly techno literate. And I'm everlastingly grateful because I wouldn't have done it on my own. Now I must pick up the gauntlet and pass on what I have learned, especially to *my people,* those 50+."

Brigid recommends the following websites:

- www.facebook.com/NextChapterNYPL/ (the New York Public Library's "Next Chapter" Facebook page for active adults at midlife or older)
- www.nypl.org/blog_user/180/ (Brigid's blog)

NOTES

1. Jennifer Osborn, "Developing Teaching and Training Skills," 2007, www.liscareer.com/osborn_training.htm.
2. Howard L. Simmons, "Librarian as Teacher: A Personal View," *College and Undergraduate Libraries* 6, no. 2 (2000): 41–44.
3. Scott Walter, "Librarians as Teachers: A Qualitative Inquiry into Professional Identity," *College and Research Libraries* 60, no. 1 (January 2008): 51–71.
4. Association of College and Research Libraries, "Standards for Proficiencies for Instruction Librarians and Coordinators," 2007, www.ala.org/ala/mgrps/divs/acrl/standards/profstandards.cfm.

CHAPTER 4

LIBRARIANS AS ENTREPRENEURS

NEVER BEFORE have there been so many opportunities in librarianship outside the traditional library setting. When the Information Age began to shake the time-honored foundations of librarianship, many in the field saw the opportunity to offer their "traditional" skills—the management, organization, and distribution of knowledge—to a much wider variety of patrons through innovative ways.

In the past, librarians rarely branched out on their own to become freelancers. That is rapidly changing. More and more librarians are taking their skills out of the library to work for themselves from home, to work for others from home (telecommuting), to form their own businesses, or to work on a contract basis for various organizations.[1] Many are attracted to the flexibility and variety that freelancing, contracting, and telecommuting can provide. Librarians with entrepreneurial interests have started their own consulting practices, acting as freelance reference librarians or information brokers and providing services to other libraries, businesses, government agencies, or the general consumer. Information architects design various systems to help people access information with as little hassle as possible. Knowledge managers identify, accumulate, and apply knowledge to further an organization's goals.[2]

Being a librarian doesn't mean that you have to work in a library. If you have an interest in working on your own, if you know your strengths and weaknesses, and if you are willing to try something new and learn from your mistakes, take the leap!

The possibilities of applying the skills you learn as a librarian to revolutionary jobs are endless.

ENVIRONMENTS

Librarians as entrepreneurs are in the unique position to formulate their own working environments, whether it be working from home, in an office building, or in a coffee shop using wireless technology. Below are a few of the areas in which librarians are finding successful freelance careers.

Indexer. Many librarians enjoy working as freelance indexers. This is one of the more natural transitions from the traditional library environment. Most library schools offer advanced indexing courses, and librarians use those indexing skills every day while cataloging, searching databases, and doing reference work. Freelance indexing can take many forms, including "back-of-the-book" indexing, abstracting, website indexing, periodicals indexing, and database indexing.

Information broker/independent researcher. Freelance information professionals are known as information brokers, freelance librarians, online searchers, or information experts. They tend to specialize in specific areas such as law, business, or medicine, and often have advanced degrees in these subjects in addition to the library degree. They provide a variety of services such as market research, competitive intelligence, and complex literature searches.

Consultant. Many librarians who have worked for years in the library field have successfully become freelance consultants. They generally target libraries for such services as strategic planning, problem solving, team building, organizational diagnosis, conflict management, process improvement, customer service, and team concepts. This type of work requires a commitment to helping libraries become better organizations.

Writer/editor. Many librarians find it natural to pursue a career in writing or editing. They may be involved with copyediting, proofreading, writing, or other editorial services. Some librarians who work as freelance indexers will also perform editing work.

Freelance cataloger. A librarian who catalogs from home on a freelance basis can find work from a variety of institutions looking to outsource their cataloging. Librarians who have taken advanced courses in subject and descriptive cataloging in library school, and who have experience with cataloging in a library setting, will find this a fairly easy transition.

24/7 reference specialist. Many organizations have begun to employ private reference librarians for 24/7 reference work. This is a great opportunity for reference librarians interested in part-time work from home.

SKILLS

Not every librarian will be successful as an entrepreneur. It takes a certain skill set and a lot of hard work and dedication to make ends meet. When first starting out, many freelance librarians devote 50–60 hours each week to launching their businesses. Business, marketing, and networking skills are a must. Below is a list of general skills necessary for a successful librarian entrepreneur:

- willingness to take risks and learn from mistakes
- business skills (accounting, marketing, networking, etc.)
- research skills
- subject expertise
- technological skills
- flexibility and adaptability
- time management and organizational skills
- communication skills, both written and verbal
- ability to connect with clients and interpret their needs
- persistence

EDUCATION AND TRAINING

Generally, a master's degree in library and information science from an ALA-accredited institution is sufficient for librarian entrepreneurs. Many freelancers, though, stress the need for specialized training in certain disciplines as well as advanced business training.

PROFESSIONAL ASSOCIATIONS

Below is a list of associations recommended by the various librarians "spotlighted" in this chapter:

- American Library Association (ALA)—www.ala.org
  - *Association of Specialized and Cooperative Library Agencies (ASCLA)* www.ala.org/ascla/
- Special Libraries Association (SLA)—www.sla.org

- Association of Independent Information Professionals (AIIP)—www.aiip.org
- ASIS&T (American Society for Information Science and Technology)—www.asis.org
- Association of Research Libraries (ARL)—www.arl.org
- Associations specific to the entrepreneur's specialty, such as the American Association of Law Libraries (AALL—www.aallnet.org) or the Medical Library Association (MLA—www.mlanet.org)

—————— SPOTLIGHTS ——————

JUDITH TAPIERO

President, The Organized Library, Baltimore, Maryland

"Librarians must be able to create new and alternative careers for themselves."

JUDITH TAPIERO has been the president of her own library consulting firm for over twenty years. Her business, The Organized Library (http://theorganizedlibrary.com), offers specialized consulting services to corporate or business libraries, special libraries, nonprofit organizations, and private collections. Throughout the years, Judith and her team have completed over 200 projects for their clients. These projects have involved strategic planning, library space planning, library organization, virtual/electronic libraries, budgeting, library staffing and development, library policies, and marketing strategy and profitability.

"We work on a wide variety of issues," Judith says. "We customize a strategy and implementation plan for each client depending on their individual needs and available resources." Her deep-seated personal mission is to "save libraries" and to do what needs to be done to stop a library from being eliminated altogether. Her firm's motto is "We don't just have ideas, we implement them."

As with most entrepreneurs who serve as their own bosses, Judith has no set schedule or standard daily responsibilities. "The timeline of a project determines what I work on each day," she explains. "A project may take one or two days, three months, or even a year. Sometimes one thing adds onto another so that if there are delays, the whole timeline can be set back. One has to account for 'contingencies' in proposals to clients."

Judith says that the most challenging, exciting, and unique features of her job all boil down to the same thing: helping a client create or restore their library to be a functioning and valued asset for their organization. "No one else does this exactly the same way as I do," she says. "The satisfaction I feel after a job is completed is immeasurable."

According to Judith, to be an entrepreneur one must first build a portfolio of skills. This can only be done through on-the-job experience. "Someone who has a 'calling' to go out on their own must put in some years in regular jobs before taking the plunge," she says. "In order to be regarded as an expert whom someone will hire, you need to have a résumé that indicates experience in that area."

Following her own advice, Judith gathered years of experience as a professional librarian before considering venturing out on her own. Her love for libraries began in childhood, where she "grew up in a house where there were always books, intellectual discussions, and, with a professor for a father, a constant buying of books." Her father had a collection of over 20,000 books in six languages on many and varied topics such as history, politics, art, religion, and philosophy. "I decided I wanted to do something with libraries as a career," she says. She received her B.A. in history from Brandeis University and her M.L.S. from Rutgers University.

After graduating from Rutgers, she did volunteer work for the community, setting up libraries at the local synagogue and community center and training others to develop and run small libraries. "At this point, going out on my own was not even on the radar," she says. "I had not really had a 'real' job yet."

Her first "real job" was at an economics consulting firm where she was hired to set up a library from scratch, run it, do research, and prepare and write analyses of the information she gathered. This job built on the volunteer experience she'd had in setting up libraries, but with the added responsibilities of administration. "I had the first computer in the firm," she says. "I used it to access early Dialog and Nexis databases. No one else had a computer on the desktop at that time, and the staff assistants who typed up the client studies and reports did not yet have computers at their desks either."

After nine years, Judith took a job at a financial consulting firm whose clients were the top fifty banks in the world. There, too, she set up their library and ran it, but they did have an automated catalog and several financial databases created in-house or purchased from outside vendors. Judith recalls two incidents at this particular job that showcased her initiative and her follow-through, and that eventually changed the "status quo" and enabled the firm to take a groundbreaking step.

The first incident involved the CFO to whom she initially reported. "He had no interest in or use for the library," she says. "He was not helpful to me; he did not mentor me nor did he champion my cause for additional library purchases or agree to more personnel. I went to the president's office after about three months and told him that I wanted to report to someone who was at least interested in the library and its future. The president asked who I would like to report to and I said him because he had hired me; he was very interested in and 'got' the importance of the library's value to the firm. He agreed. Every week for the three years I was there, we sat down and talked strategy about the library. He trusted me and listened to my suggestions and plans for growing the library."

The second incident involved staff requests for information too close to contractual deadlines. "This happened fairly often," Judith says. "At the last minute before a project was due, someone would inevitably ask for a research initiative that needed more than a day to complete." She asked the president if she could begin attending the initial project meetings of the staff with the clients at their bank in order to take notes on the types of research that would be needed for the project, as well as to be able to understand all the different project components. This would eliminate a "last-minute rush" for information. "This request was revolutionary to the consulting world," Judith explains. "Only principals usually went to the initial project meetings. Even the VPs and associates were not 'invited' to attend. The president agreed to a trial period. We were the first firm to initiate this policy as part of the project management procedure. It worked very well."

These experiences validated the risks Judith took in stepping forward, speaking up, and creating an atmosphere for change. "These would later help me in spotting the areas of change that needed to be addressed with my own clients," she explains.

After three years, Judith felt that she had gone as far as she could go in the company. "Rather than going to a competitor and doing the same thing, I knew I was ready to go out on my own," she says. "Now was the time and I should do it or regret it forever. During my career I slowly worked my way toward entrepreneurship and one day I had that 'aha' moment when I realized with clarity that this was the direction I had to take."

Thanks to her years of experience, Judith has a lot of advice for librarians who have an interest in independent consulting. She maintains that not all librarians have the combination of innate and learned abilities to become successful entrepreneurs. For those who do manage to venture out on their own successfully, there are several common denominators. "They must be able to work independently—to be their own boss," she says. "They must have the confidence to direct their own career path with no guidance from above. They must be confident in their ability to do a job to a client's satisfaction. They must be detail-oriented. They must have a 'guiding mission' which was the reason for them to go out on their own in the first place. They must be able to market themselves and their services. They must be able to hire good people to assist in the consulting process. They must enjoy networking, being in public, teaching workshops, giving speeches, and making presentations to management. They should be individuals who do not mind being in the limelight." She goes on to say that, unfortunately, our profession tends to attract people more interested in intellectual challenges than in being in the limelight. "This is where the disconnect lies," she says. "Until we can draw to the profession the types of people who will combine both of these skills and abilities, we will be facing an uphill battle."

Judith says that the key to her success as a consultant has been her marketing efforts to clients. "Since I was not good at speaking to bodiless voices on the telephone, I hired a telemarketer nineteen years ago who continues to find leads for me. I am very good at what I do but marketing was never a forte of mine, and I suspect the same is true for many librarians." She encourages people to take business courses while in library school. "Business schools offer marketing, strategic planning, finance, and other courses that will orient you to the workplace at large and the library's place within the company," she says. "These are key for helping to integrate the library into the overall mission of the organization and making it part of the planning/budget process. Librarians never had to do this before and are finding out—sometimes too late—that their lack of skills at promoting their own value, as well as their inability to show the value contributed by the library to the bottom line (using tools such as annual reports, quarterly statistics, or board presentations), often hastens the library's demise and their being laid off as well. 'Budget cuts' are often an excuse by management to mask performance issues, maximization of resources, and not enough demonstrated value."

Judith admits that she does not have enough time to keep up with changing technologies. To assist her with this, she partners with a technology firm that deals with libraries. "I call them in if a project involves digitizing resources, records management, coordinating or working with in-house databases, intranets, e-management, etc.," she says. She does attend professional conferences but tends to focus on the strategic planning sessions, the exhibits, and the networking events. She is a member of the Special Libraries Association and serves as a director of the Maryland Chapter. In that capacity, she works on fostering the relationships between the chapter and the iSchool

(College of Information Studies) students at the University of Maryland. She is also a member of the Leadership and Management Division and the Consulting Section within SLA. To those first starting out in business, Judith recommends joining the Association of Independent Information Professionals, an entrepreneurial group that includes many librarians who run their own businesses (www.aiip.org).

In conclusion, Judith makes a pitch for alternative and innovative careers for librarians. "Today, the traditional careers in librarianship are few and far between," she says. "The profession has evolved and changed so quickly and drastically in the last ten years. Librarians—not usually known for their adaptability, initiative, flexibility, and innovation—must be able to do all these things at the drop of a hat or they will lose their jobs, the jobs will disappear, and the profession will die. Librarians must be able to create new and alternative careers for themselves, and to form new niches within their own companies and organizations."

For more information about Judith and her company, visit The Organized Library at http://theorganizedlibrary.com.

AMELIA KASSEL

President, MarketingBase, Sebastopol, California

"The best feature of my job is the creative nature of owning and operating a business."

WHILE IT is true that millions of people do their own Internet research (who doesn't know how to "Google"?), there are many professionals in various fields who simply don't have the time or the skills to do their own research. So where do these professionals go when they need online research? They seek out the uniquely specialized services offered by librarian entrepreneurs like Amelia Kassel, who has worked as an independent information professional for over twenty-five years.

Amelia is the president and owner of MarketingBase, a firm specializing in industry, company, and competitive and market intelligence research (www.marketingbase .com/index.html). Her clients span all industries and range from individual consultants to large corporations. She has worked on hundreds of projects since establishing her information brokerage in 1982, most often dealing with business research such as industry, market, or company research as well as other business topics. For example, she has done work for both law and health-related firms, including applications for market research, competitive intelligence, marketing, new product introduction, and mergers and acquisitions.

Amelia's daily professional routine is not set in stone. She serves as her own boss and therefore has the flexibility to determine her own schedule. "I do all my work online," she says. "A routine day starts with checking e-mail, reviewing newsletter alerts, and responding to clients and colleagues. I participate in many discussion lists and strive to keep up with them. Other tasks of a typical day will vary from working on deadline questions for clients to doing some of the administrative work needed to operate a business."

In addition to running her business, Amelia spends a lot of time writing, consulting, and teaching. "I began giving presentations, workshops, and seminars in the '80s," she says, "and today travel within the United States and internationally to conferences to train librarians and business searchers on the skills they need to conduct market and competitive intelligence research." She has taught courses on information brokering and on alternative careers to LIS students at San José State University. She has given countless speeches and presentations at various national and international conferences and professional venues on topics such as demonstrating value, competitive intelligence, business research tactics, writing marketing plans, building a successful information business, cost-effective research, and using the Internet for effective research. She is the author of *The Super Searchers on Wall Street* (www.supersearchers.com) and writes for industry publications such as *Searcher* magazine (www.infotoday.com/searcher/default.asp).

On top of everything else, Amelia runs a successful training and mentoring program for new independent information professionals, information brokers, and business researchers. The Mentor Program (http://marketingbase.com/mentor.html) is a yearlong, self-paced, one-on-one program that is tailored to each student based on his or her interests and requirements. Students learn about setting up their own businesses, the ins and outs of worldwide database searching, market planning and strategies, and all the other essentials required for new information professionals to succeed on their own.

"Working independently is enormously satisfying, because you do what you enjoy," Amelia says. However, she did not envision a career as an independent information professional until she had been in the workforce for a while. After receiving her B.A. in anthropology at California State University, she followed in her sister's footsteps and received her master of library science degree from the University of California at Los Angeles (UCLA). She was awarded a predoctoral fellowship funded by the National Library of Medicine and was among four interns at the UCLA Biomedical Library for one year. During the fellowship she rotated through all the library departments, including acquisitions, cataloging, and reference. She also spent time working with the Pacific Southwest Regional Medical Library Service (PSRMLS), which offered consulting and training to medical libraries in four states. When the internship was complete, the UCLA Biomedical Library hired her full-time. She divided her time between interlibrary loans and PSRMLS services, where she trained hospital librarians on how to write grant applications and how to establish health care collections for physicians and allied health care professionals. This first professional position gave Amelia a taste for non-traditional work. Though she was based in a library, she traveled to libraries in the region to provide on-site workshops and consulting.

After three years, Amelia moved to northern California and became an adult reference librarian for the Sonoma County Public Library. Eight years later she became the reference coordinator for the North Bay Cooperative Library System (NBCLS), a multi-type library system that includes public and academic libraries, based within the Sonoma County Public Library. "Again, I found myself working in an alternative or non-traditional job," she says. "I provided reference service to libraries in the region and coordinated continuing education programs for librarians in the system."

It was during that time that Amelia was exposed to online services. "We established an account with Dialog," she says. "All adult reference librarians were trained by an on-site Dialog trainer. When first introduced to Dialog, I was absolutely wowed. It opened up a whole new world of knowledge, much like what the Internet has done today." Later that year, she began to consider establishing an information brokerage business based on skills she had learned as a librarian.

"While attending a conference at the California Library Association," she explains, "I chanced across an exhibitor, Sue Rugge, who was demonstrating how her company (Information on Demand) conducted online searches for clients. I immediately decided that this was what I would like to do."

Knowing that she needed new skills to start a business, Amelia enrolled in business classes at the local community college, where she learned about business planning, marketing, and sales. She continued to hone her online research skills. She established her online information brokerage in 1982 while still working at NBCLS. In 1984 she resigned from her job and went into business full-time.

Amelia says that there are a variety of skills one must have in order to be successful as an independent information professional. "You need to be proficient at online research skills, and you need to have people skills," she says. "You must have evaluative and critical thinking skills, as well as the personality traits of independence, flexibility, adaptability, creativity, and problem solving." In addition, one needs to have the skills necessary to operate a small business and to market and sell services effectively.

Amelia is constantly learning new skills. "As an information entrepreneur, I enjoy variety," she says. "I'm a generalist because of my background and interests, which permits me to research just about any topic or industry." Many of the new skills she learns are customer-driven. When a customer asks for something she hasn't done before, she assesses her skills and usually determines that she can meet the need. She may have an initial learning curve, but is always able to satisfy her clients and gain their respect and trust. By constantly expanding her acquired knowledge in this manner, she is able to widen her range of services.

Since information entrepreneurs are so dependent on resources driven by technology, it is important to stay abreast of technological developments and new trends in the industry. Amelia accomplishes this by attending conferences, participating in electronic discussion forums, and engaging in independent learning. She networks with colleagues and prospective new clients at meetings and through social networks facilitated by Web 2.0 technology such as LinkedIn and Twitter.

"Since the start of my career, I've been able to put my graduate library education and a range of experiences to work to create an alternative career," Amelia says. "Today, there is nothing I love more than imparting some of my knowledge to others embarking on new careers. By keeping current, staying focused, and adapting to new technology and customer needs, I've been able to work in an alternative career for more than twenty-five years. By combining skills, dedication, and drive, you too can do what you love."

To learn more about Amelia and about being an independent information professional, visit:

- www.marketingbase.com/index.html (MarketingBase, Amelia's business)
- www.aiip.org (Association of Independent Information Professionals)

Note: Portions of this interview were derived from the following articles:

- "Alternative Careers," Amelia Kassel (http://lisjobs.com/career_trends/?p=316)
- "The Evolution of Information Brokering: A Career Alternative for Librarians and Info Pros," Amelia Kassel (http://lisjobs.com/career_trends/?p=476)

NANCY K. HUMPHREYS

CEO, Wordmaps Indexing, Richmond, California

"Those in business for themselves wear two hats: employee and employer."

NANCY HUMPHREYS holds master's degrees in English, economics, and library science. The career path she has chosen is a unique blend of all three areas of study. As a freelance indexer, she is able to use her English and library science backgrounds to enhance her indexing skills and her economics background to handle the nitty-gritty details of running a business.

Nancy is the chief executive officer of Wordmaps Indexing (www.wordmapsindexing.com). In this capacity, she creates indexes "that promote the goals of authors and publishers, whether it's to make money, make a name, earn fame, or entertain." Her website boasts an impressive list of books she has indexed, including biographies, business and career titles, catalogs, college textbooks, computer texts, cookbooks, guidebooks, programming books, scholarly works, and magazines or journals. The "Wordmaps" concept stems from the parallel between maps and indexing: just as a map is a representation of a larger area on a much smaller scale, an index uses words and concepts to represent the content of a book.

Nancy did not begin her career as a freelance indexer. It took twenty years of working for others before she finally settled into her own indexing business. She received her master's degrees in English and economics from the University of Wisconsin at Madison. After a few years, during the recession of the mid-1970s, she enrolled in the School of Librarianship at the University of South Carolina in Columbia. "I chose the library school because I liked the pioneering idea of the department's single team-taught twelve-credit course for the first semester," she says. "Only after being there for a semester did we all discover that the second semester featured 'modular units' that would be taught by one professor, and we students would work as teams! We learned we'd be graded as a group, not as individuals, in each class. The panic that day was palpable. The building almost lifted off the ground." She goes on to explain that the "modular units" were based on NASA research showing the superiority of groups in decision-making. "I loved it," she continues. "It was a great experience that I've carried with me through my career."

Nancy completed a library internship at the Richland County Public Library in Columbia, South Carolina. She then worked for ten years at the University of Wisconsin at LaCrosse as a business bibliographer and reference librarian. Later, she moved to Berkeley where she held two positions at the University of California, Berkeley: first she ran the Women's Center library for three years, and then served for two years as a reference librarian at the main graduate student library on campus. While there, she worked weekends at the Oakland Public Library. Finally, she worked for two nonprofit organizations in San Francisco and Marin County.

"I began thinking of working for myself about ten years after becoming a librarian," Nancy says. "But it took me another ten years to get the nerve to strike out on my own. I tried computer consulting, abstracting, database searching, and finally settled into indexing."

Since she is self-employed, Nancy has no set daily routine. "Sometimes I wish there were!" she says. In addition to the actual tasks involved with indexing, she spends a lot of time working on the management side of her business. Her article entitled "How Many Hats Do You Wear?" lists a variety of tasks and duties involved with being self-employed (http://brucenomics.com/?p=5#more-5). Since she serves as "employer" as well as "employee" in her own business, she must act as her own director, marketer, business manager, receptionist, accountant/bookkeeper, computer technician, and maintenance worker, to name a few.

"My primary clients are authors who wish to self-publish," says Nancy. "I have gradually moved away from the traditional publishing world and toward the new Internet model for authors and other creative people called 'self-publishing, self-promotion, and self-distribution.'" She has indexed the works of a Hollywood location scout, an English teacher who wrote a mathematical physics book, two gay ministers fostering the idea of "welcoming congregations," and the chronicler of sailing clubs around the world.

Her secondary clients are businesspersons (attorneys, importers, computer sales companies, insurance companies), traditional publishers (scholarly, trade, library, and how-to guide publishers), and others who need indexing services (nonprofit organizations, research institutes, and trade associations).

"The best part of my job is the sales part," Nancy says. "I like meeting new people and getting to talk about what they want to accomplish." She works closely with each client during the Wordmaps process, which includes five steps. These are (1) identify the goals of the author and publisher; (2) define the primary and secondary audiences for the book; (3) match the content and style of the index to that of the book; (4) whenever necessary, use the index to correct weaknesses in the book; and (5) always make sure the index maps the strengths of the book.

Over the years, technology has changed the indexing profession. "I began my indexing career with a box of index cards and a two-foot sorting device with A–Z flaps," Nancy explains. "When the first PCs came out, I paid $2,000 for an IBM with one floppy drive and a green monochrome monitor. It took all evening and sometimes all night to sort an index, but it speeded my work immensely. I loved it. Now I use a Mac Air along with a twenty-four-inch screen in my work. I have a printer, but indexers are now working with .pdf files rather than paper." She uses special indexing software and is currently exploring new software for indexing on the Internet.

Specialized training is important for indexers. "American library schools did not offer courses on indexing when I received my degree," Nancy says. "That is now changing." She received her official training in indexing from the British Society of Indexers via the Rapid Results College in London in 1984. "These days, though, indexing courses are offered by the U.S. Department of Agriculture, the American Society for Indexing (ASI), as well as many local institutions, including library schools."

To keep up with changes in her field, Nancy attends ASI workshops and classes offered by the local PASS group (an organization of online virtual assistants). "Along with core indexing skills, learning new skills is essential for self-employed workers," she says. She is a member of ASI and the Feral Workers of America. In the past, she has been involved in the American Library Association and the Special Libraries Association. She participates in electronic discussion lists and a social network for indexers on Ning.com.

In her "spare time" Nancy writes professional articles on entrepreneurship, economics, and other topics, and she has often presented at professional meetings. She also enjoys writing fiction and has won several literary awards. She is currently working on a book of short stories called *Other Realities.*

"There are not a lot of librarians who are professional indexers," says Nancy. "But librarians have a lot of different skills. All are useful in indexing. Indexing requires the combined skills learned in both technical service and reference librarianship."

Nancy holds that librarians today should become actively involved in the new online world of information and knowledge sharing. "I think we are at the beginning of a new economic era," she says. "Current financial and economic factors are bringing about the new Internet business model of self-publishing, self-promotion, and self-distribution. I hope librarians play a part in that." She advises people interested in a career like hers to look at business models like the "1,000 True Fans" model and the Artists Services Model as described in David Mathison's book *Be the Media* (www .bethemedia.com/index.html).

"I view myself as an entrepreneur as well as a freelancer," Nancy concludes. "I encourage librarians to pursue both things—self-employment as a freelancer and innovation through entrepreneurship. Pensions and Social Security may not be available at retirement time as they are today. Librarians had better be successful at more than jobs."

For more information about indexing or entrepreneurship, Nancy recommends the following sites:

- www.wordmapsindexing.com (her business website)
- http://brucenomics.com (Nancy's entrepreneurship/economics blog)
- http://creatingwebsuccess.com (Creating Web Success)

ALEXANDER H. COHEN

Library Consultant, Aaron Cohen Associates, Ltd., Croton-on-Hudson, New York

"The only way to succeed is to believe in the work you do."

WHAT KIND of librarian do you get when you combine (a) a B.S. in finance, (b) a master's in library science, (c) a strong IT background, (d) expertise in knowledge management, and (e) a family with more than thirty years of experience in library planning, design, and consultation? The answer: you get a highly effective library management consultant specializing in Web 2.0 library spaces. In short, you get Alexander Cohen.

Alex Cohen is a library consultant with Aaron Cohen Associates, Ltd., an interdisciplinary library-planning firm founded in 1972. He is one of a team of ten library planners, librarians, architects, materials management experts, interior designers, and organizational management consultants, all of whom specialize in library service planning and design. Over the years, the firm has worked for hundreds of libraries on new building projects, reorganization of effort, and renovation of services, always with a focus on organizational efficiency.

"As a library planner, my duty is to make my clients happy," Alex says. "I understand it is a cliché, but I like to be challenged with innovative people and ideas. In our work, we become partners with librarians. We explore their skills and leverage their experience to meet the unique needs of the libraries we work on." His clients are librarians from academic, public, governmental, special, and medical libraries. In his fifteen years of experience as a management consultant, he has worked on both large and small projects involving organizational development, strategic planning, classroom design, usage studies, distributed learning, grant writing, focus groups, Internet and IT systems integration, and knowledge management applications. His extensive technology experience allows him to focus on library planning and technical design within the context of Web 2.0 environments. "My typical responsibilities include project management, report writing, and—most importantly—library space planning and digital research," he says.

"I don't live a normal 9-to-5 life," Alex says. He works six days a week and does a lot of traveling. "I typically do a two-day site visit to a library, so this takes me to many places and time zones. When I am on-site, I am a library researcher. All of my attention is on the library and its community. I interview and listen to as many people as I can, and try to learn as much as I can within the time scheduled. This is usually an 8-a.m.-to-9-p.m. day that includes presentations, note taking, and discussions."

Traveling is one of the most challenging features of Alex's job. "I love to travel," he says, "but it takes a special person to be adaptable in different cultures. Sometimes you are dropped into communities that are very different and you have to be patient and polite." When he is not traveling, he works from his home office and therefore gets to spend a little more time with his family.

Alex's unique job is not lacking in other challenges as well. "Being a library researcher takes a lot of organization," he explains. He wears many different hats and takes on a variety of tasks, including paperwork and running all the IT systems. A particular challenge is the need to "show value" in the first exchange with a library or client. "When I wasn't as experienced as I am today, this was very difficult. You can't make everyone your friend all the time. You need patience to provide consulting support." He goes on to explain that sometimes a project requires him to take a stand on something. "My father always says that it is better to take a stand than to allow things to get out of control. We provide value even when no one wants to hear it, and we are willing to go to the mat if necessary. Obviously, this needs to be done delicately and politely."

Library planning and consulting seem to run in Alex's family. "My parents, Aaron and Elaine Cohen, wrote three books on library planning and design," he explains. "They traveled the world building libraries for communities. They were an inspiration to me growing up. From 1972 to 2000, they worked on over 300 library projects and did over 1,000 workshops on library space planning and design." Alex likes to tell people that his family has a library of library plans consisting of over forty years of research.

"My family has done many innovative projects," he continues. "Though the methodology is always the same, all of the projects have been different. There is no one library plan that is the same as another, because each library is different and special.

Each library has inimitable users and staff, a unique community and location, and distinctive collections and services."

Despite the familial interest in libraries and consulting, Alex did not initially set out to become a library consultant. After earning his B.S. in finance at the University of Arizona, he found himself interested in the media and went to Hollywood to learn about film and music. He worked as an assistant to the producer for several films, then moved to northern California to take advantage of the media revolution. "During the 1990s, it was a great time to be innovative with technology, but also a hard time to get a job with no experience in computers," he recounts. "After going through a list of media companies, I found a job working for Red Dot Interactive in Multimedia Gulch. This was a very exciting place. We worked to develop multimedia content for Global 100 businesses. We developed some of the first Internet sites for big business." Thus began Alex's extensive experience in technology.

Alex got married, moved to London, and found himself running an Internet studio. After two years, he moved again to an American company—USWeb/CKS—and became a management consultant in information technology. "I started building Internet/intranets for large organizations including Unilever, Norwich Union, British Gas, Thomas Cook, and Eurotunnel. I led a project team that tested the first version of Microsoft SharePoint."

It was during that time that Alex realized the information systems he was developing were like libraries. "Technology was playing a role to connect personal and research data," he explains. "While working on a project, I started to use SharePoint as a content management system. I also learned about digital content and the need for a catalog to connect all the disparate pieces together."

Later, Alex moved to San Francisco to "join a dot-com and make my millions (so I thought)." He joined a project funded by the French post office and led a team to develop drop ship centers. "These were places where people could buy something online and get it delivered to a store near the customer," he explains. "The store was a bit like a private library; people would buy something and then they would use the store to gather their stuff. Somehow in my eyes, the whole project was like a library. Unfortunately, UPS and FedEx developed their own stores and the dot-com didn't have a chance."

The dot-com business went bust. "It happened very fast and was devastating to everyone. I had a family of four to feed and no way to pay the bills. There were no jobs for a technology manager without a master's degree. There was no way to find a job in that climate. At the same time, my parents were looking to retire. They were still working on libraries, but my mom (Elaine Cohen) wanted to retire."

Alex moved back to New York and, with the help of his father, became engaged in a large renovation project at Long Island University. "But there was one thing missing," he says. "I didn't have a library degree." He enrolled in the Library and Information School at the university. "The university librarian, David Ungarelli, became my mentor, and the dean of the Library and Information School, Michael Koenig, energized my academic spirit. Michael was a very intelligent knowledge management specialist whose books on libraries expanded my vision of what libraries will be in the future. My father, Aaron Cohen, also pushed me to learn more about the future of libraries (online reading rooms, content management, asset management). This is how I became the library consultant that I am today."

Alex uses his IT experience as a supplement to his daily work. He developed the company website (www.acohen.com) and used his knowledge to link into search engines and to develop links to relevant information. "Everything I do online links into our work as library planners," he says. "I got onto Second Life to learn about virtual worlds, and I became involved with Facebook to get involved online socially. Both experiences support my day job."

To keep up with changes in the field, Alex is a member of the American Library Association, the Association of College and Research Libraries, the Special Libraries Association, and the International Federation of Library Associations. He utilizes the newsletters and the research from each of these associations to support his planning studies. "I have gone to every ALA [conference] since 2002," he says. "At first it was difficult since I didn't know anyone and I don't have a traditional job. Some librarians think of me as a vendor. I am and I am not. People seek us out; I never look for clients at professional conferences. Instead, I go to conferences to learn about the latest and greatest changes in the industry."

Alex maintains that librarians must be flexible in the future. "We must be researchers, advocates, and teachers," he says. "We must focus on making our services useful and simple. All of the work I have done has focused on simplicity. I use technology to support simple operations, enabling librarians to do less clerical/manual work and more abstract work.

"Librarians are on the cutting edge of change," he continues. "They need to ask questions like: Should there be any books in a library? Do we need a library building? What is the library of the future going to look like? Librarians should develop options, scenarios, and discussion points to support service goals and objectives. Librarians have special skills to research and collate results. They are organized and flexible and unflappable. In an organization, librarians can be anything they want to be—research support, a friendly face . . . or the foundation and the innovator."

Alex says that though technology is part of the future, the real driving force is the people. "Throughout my career I have always tried to find out how people are using a library to deliver better services. While technology can play a role in developing stronger operational efficiencies, it is an organization's staff who define its future."

To those interested in becoming freelance consultants, Alex says, "If you aren't organized, take a 9-to-5 job. It's easier. The most effective freelancers are the ones who are organized. You have to be flexible in the types of work you do. Go after your dream clients, but remember that the small guy is the one who will pay you when the going gets rough. The most important skill is listening. The second is confidence."

"As librarians, we are all researchers at heart," Alex concludes. "I love to find things and to make sure they work. I enjoy finding new ways to provide services and adapting spaces to respond to those services. I will take on any project that is innovative and strategic," Alex concludes. "You should, too."

Alex recommends the following websites:

- www.acohen.com (Aaron Cohen Associates, Ltd.)
- www.clir.org (Council on Library and Information Resources)
- www.oclc.org (a worldwide library cooperative)

BILL WILSON

Partner, Himmel and Wilson, Library Consultants, Milton, Wisconsin

"You have to be a bit of a risk taker to be an entrepreneur in the library field. Believing that you will succeed is essential in taking the leap."

WHAT COULD possibly motivate a librarian to leave a solid position—complete with a regular paycheck, health insurance, and a pension—for the uncertainty of consulting? Bill Wilson's answer would be, "I saw the opportunity for helping real people reach their full potential."

Helping libraries to "reach their full potential" is a large part of Bill Wilson's job. As a library consultant for Himmel and Wilson (http://my.execpc.com/~himmel/), he and his partner, Ethel Himmel, assist all types of libraries with their planning, technology, management, and building needs. Together, they have completed nearly 200 projects with libraries, library systems, and state library agencies in forty states.

"When you cut to the chase, a consultant's major job duty is problem solving," Bill says. "Our firm tries to approach every new project without preconceived notions of what solution is appropriate in a given situation. What works in one place may not work in another due to factors as diverse as governance structure, sources of funding, staff skills, etc."

Bill says that the daily work of a consultant varies depending upon his or her role in a particular project. Each project may be vastly different from another. "People hire consultants for a wide variety of reasons," he explains. "The client may not be sure of the direction their library should go, or they may simply be looking for outside validation of the soundness of a direction that is under consideration. Occasionally, a consultant plays the important role of being the bearer of bad news." He says that sometimes the consultant may have to "take the heat" for introducing unpopular, but necessary, realities.

Himmel and Wilson caters to two distinct client groups: public libraries and state library agencies. "Although we work with regional library systems and cooperatives and have done some work for federal agencies such as the Institute of Museum and Library Services, public libraries and state library agencies account for the majority of our business," says Bill.

The education level of their clientele varies significantly. They have worked with some small public libraries directed by individuals with less than bachelor's degrees. On the other hand, they have also worked for clients who held multiple master's degrees and doctorates. "Although we encounter clients with a wide variety of educational attainment, service philosophies, and compensation levels," Bill says, "the unifying characteristic is that most are highly committed to their work and believe that libraries change lives."

According to Bill, an important aspect of consulting that many people neglect to consider is that "part of the job is getting the next job." Consultants must have the ability to market themselves and attract clients. "Most of the projects that our firm undertakes are the result of being selected through a competitive bidding process," he explains. "Understanding what a potential client really wants and needs and crafting a proposal that is highly responsive is an important part of what consultants do. Clients almost never compensate consultants for time spent developing proposals. Yet this task can occupy a considerable amount of time. While consultants' billing rates often seem high, they need to reflect non-billable time, costs related to benefits, costs related to liability insurance, and a host of other business expenses that aren't always obvious."

Bill says that the most exciting feature of being a library consultant is the opportunity to meet and interact with "real people" throughout the nation. "We have encountered people ranging from Somali immigrants to millionaire entrepreneurs and from homeschooled second graders to published authors in focused groups," he explains. "We've interviewed futurists and historians, elected officials, and food stamp recipients in the course of gathering background information."

For him, another exciting facet of his work is travel. "Our firm has been involved in projects in forty states over the course of the last two decades," he says. "Spending time in large cities and small towns in Oregon, Florida, Maine, and California can be enjoyable and often provides unique insights into the American psyche." There are downsides to frequent travel, however. "Getting to these far-flung destinations has become increasingly unpleasant. Both my business partner and I were in the air on separate planes on the morning of September 11, 2001. Flying 50,000–100,000 miles per year and spending up to 100 nights per year in hotels isn't all it's cracked up to be!"

When asked about the development of his career, Bill replies, "In a way, my career found me rather than my setting out to find a career." He was introduced to working in libraries when he got a job as a "page" at age fifteen in a neighborhood public library in Buffalo, New York. "I was looking for a way to earn some spending money," he says. "Both my sister and my cousins had worked at the neighborhood branch library after school, so I knew they hired high school students. Forty-five years later, I'm still working with libraries!"

Bill says, "I started looking for a job and ended up finding a career." An important turning point for him was the day he was introduced to the new assistant branch manager. The fact that impressed him was that the new assistant branch manager was a man. "Before that time I had never considered librarianship as a career for a man," he explains.

"I headed off to college out-of-state and landed a job at the college library," he continues. "I still wasn't really thinking of librarianship as a career, but the college library director encouraged me to consider library school." Though he wasn't quite convinced, he ended up in a trainee program at the Buffalo and Erie County Public Library while enrolled in the M.L.S. program at SUNY at Buffalo. "By this point I had come to appreciate the important role that libraries, particularly public libraries, can play in the lives of real people. My work in branch libraries, and subsequently in extension/outreach services, cemented the idea that library work was important."

After receiving his M.L.S., Bill worked in a series of administrative positions in municipal, county, and state government (including serving as Wisconsin's state librarian), all of which gave him the opportunity to understand how libraries function within a political context. His post-master's degree studies in urban and regional planning offered a new perspective regarding the library's role as a partner and collaborator in a democratic society. "In short," he says, "the breadth of my experiences and an increasing awareness of the important role that public libraries can play as a center of community life combined to place me in the fortunate position of having something to offer as a consultant. Practical experience working in public libraries and in a state library agency added credibility with the two major categories of entities that would become our client base."

Over the years, Bill has witnessed how technology has transformed the work of consultants. His firm was established in 1987, when e-mail, the Internet, and wireless technology weren't a factor. "Since then," he says, "technology has impacted our consulting practice in two fundamental ways. The first is simply the speed and sheer quantity of communication. Clients can ask questions and receive answers in the middle of the night. Our firm (and the libraries with which we work) has moved from the age of snail mail and fax machines to the age of BlackBerries and Facebook, all within the span of two decades.

"The second impact of technology has been in the area of innovation," he continues. "Technology affords consultants the possibility of a competitive edge in the same way it offers libraries opportunities for positioning themselves to be indispensable. In the case of our firm, innovations such as offering web-based surveys, the use of geographic information systems software to assist in the analysis of library service areas, and teleconferences and webinars have proven to be the added value that maintains a competitive edge." Bill often uses interactive web-based surveys as a method for collecting information. Web-based postings are used as a mechanism to share draft reports with planning committees and clients. In addition, he and his business partner follow some blogs with interest.

"When I was in library school, I embraced the idea that libraries were more than just books," Bill says. "I took all of the courses in 'AV' that I could squeeze in. The full scope of what computers would mean to libraries was really unknown. We knew that computers would have an impact but we really weren't sure exactly how. Later, I was fortunate enough to work with people who encouraged exploration and innovation, and this enabled me to contribute to the libraries I worked for in unique ways. When desktop computing came along, it was often the AV people who did some of the initial exploration. My exploration of computers advanced my career, and the positive feedback I received for my efforts increased my confidence and my sense that I could contribute to the profession."

Bill continues to keep up with changing technologies in the field. "I'm a gadget guy," he admits. "I'm always looking for the next technological toy and trying to figure out how that new device or new technology applies to libraries and information transfer." He attends professional conferences and is a member of several organizations such as the American Library Association, the Public Library Association, the Association of Specialized and Cooperative Library Agencies, and the Wisconsin Library Association. He is also a member of an informal organization comprised of library consultants that meets at the ALA's Annual and Midwinter conferences.

"Staying ahead of the curve requires watching what innovators and leaders are doing and breaking out of narrow, library-profession-only, constraints," says Bill. "I relish the opportunity to serve on panels with innovators and futurists. I find that this kind of interaction is very educational."

Bill feels that his practical experience as well as his library education have prepared him well for his career. "The specifics haven't been nearly as important as the philosophy of service and the principles that I gained in library school," he says. "Anyone who believes that an academic program alone will prepare them for a profession will be sadly disappointed. One gains their education by testing the principles they garner from their formal education in the 'school of hard knocks.' I learned a great deal in the library schools at SUNY at Buffalo and the University of Wisconsin Library School. However, the most important aspect of what these schools offered me was that they prepared me to continue to learn from clients like the Public Library of Youngstown and Mahoning County and the Oregon State Library."

Bill says that successful library consultants need to enjoy working with people and need to care about community. "While there are certainly specific tasks that a library consultant performs that don't directly involve human contact and human context, the bottom line is really facilitating the interaction of people with relevant information."

To those interested in a consulting career, Bill says, "Don't be afraid to try new things and don't get too comfortable in any one job. I'm a much better consultant because I held a variety of different positions. The longest I stayed in one position prior to becoming a full-time consultant was seven years. Early in my career, I was laid off during a major economic downturn. In retrospect, it was one of the best things that ever happened to me in that I was forced to try something new. While I won't go so far as to recommend unemployment, some job changing is healthy preparation for someone who aspires to become a consultant." He says that in order to have credibility, you need to have worked in some responsible positions for a while. "Once you decide to leave a regular position (with its paycheck, health insurance, and pension), I think that confidence is key," Bill concludes. "Believing that you'll succeed (or at least believing that if you don't succeed, you'll easily find another job) is essential in taking the leap."

Bill recommends the following websites:

- http://scanblog.blogspot.com (*It's All Good*—a blog from five OCLC staff about all things present and future that impact libraries and library users)
- www.techsoupforlibraries.org/?q=blog/ (*Tech Soup for Libraries*—a technology blog for libraries)

NOTES

1. Gillian Davis, "The Entrepreneurial Librarian," 2001, www.suite101.com/article.cfm/librarians_information_science/58818.
2. Laura Kane, "Careers and Environments," in *The Portable MLIS: Insights from the Experts* (Westport, CT: Libraries Unlimited, 2008).

CHAPTER 5

LIBRARIANS AS ADMINISTRATORS

BECOMING A top-level administrator is not an automatic career goal for most librarians. Many of those in the field advance steadily throughout their careers yet stop short of reaching a library directorship position or similar administrative slot. For many, this is an acceptable choice. Not everyone is "cut out" to be an administrator; the old adage "you either have it or you don't" is certainly applicable here. There are those individuals, however, who seem to be cut from a unique mold, one perfectly suited to positions of management and—more importantly—leadership. These are the people who tend to plan each step of their careers with the ultimate goal of directorship in mind.

A library administrator—whether a director, deputy director, associate director, assistant manager, or department head—has the authority and responsibility for the planning, direction, and operation of a library or a group of libraries. Regardless of the type of library involved—public, academic, school, corporate—the administrator plays a key role in shaping the library and determining its function within the institution or the community it serves. The administrator establishes the library's mission and goals and works to ensure that all library activities support those goals. He or she oversees all planning processes, manages the budget, authorizes expenditures, and oversees financial planning and fund-raising efforts. Above all, the administrator (especially the director) is the most visible and vocal representative of the library as a whole and must strive to represent and protect the library's interests within the institution as well as to outside organizations.

One of the most important responsibilities of an administrator is to provide leadership and direction to library staff. It is not enough to be a great manager. Some librarians who have worked in middle management positions with great success are frustrated to find that upper-level administration is quite different and requires a unique skill set.[1] Being a "leader"—motivating employees with self-confidence and vision, while fostering healthy respect—is not easy.

As the majority of current library directors and upper-level administrators reach retirement age in the near future, there will be many opportunities for librarians in the workforce to move into administrative positions. The library world is already calling for experienced librarians to take on the vital roles of leadership and to help shape the future of librarianship. Are you ready for the challenge?

ENVIRONMENTS

Library administrators can be found in all types and sizes of institutions, from the smallest elementary school media center to the largest research library in academia. Whether you are responsible for two part-time staff members in a tiny hospital library or 200 library employees in five branches, you will have a lot of work to do. Rest assured, though, that it is rare to find a library administrator who does not get some measure of fulfillment and satisfaction from their work.

RESPONSIBILITIES

Below are some common duties of a library director:

- Establish the library's mission, goals, and objectives and ensure that all library activities support them
- Oversee the library's planning processes, including strategic planning and building expansion and renovation
- Provide leadership and direction toward the improvement of policies and services
- Authorize policy changes that affect library users
- Prepare the annual budget, authorize expenditures, and supervise financial planning and fund-raising efforts
- Supervise and evaluate library managers; provide guidance and direction in matters relating to personnel, public relations, planning, publicity, and reporting

- Oversee and guide the recruitment, selection, and evaluation of professional library staff and authorize appointments, salaries, and terminations
- Represent the library's interest to internal and external communities
- Participate in collaborative endeavors with other libraries or institutions
- Maintain a high level of professional competence by keeping abreast of developments in librarianship and technology
- Contribute to the profession of librarianship through service, presentations, or publications

SKILLS

Effective leadership depends largely upon the leader's ability to solve the kinds of complex social problems that arise in organizations.[2] In addition to career experience, a successful administrator must demonstrate excellence in the following skills and personality attributes:

- leadership and motivational skills
- vision
- creative problem solving
- communication skills
- social judgment skills
- consensus-building skills
- political skills
- self-confidence
- decision-making skills
- intuition
- knowledge
- persistence
- networking skills

EDUCATION AND TRAINING

Experience is the key to success as a library director or administrator. Most positions require a minimum of 5–10 years of experience with progressively greater administrative responsibilities. A director, in particular, should have a rich background of knowledge and experience in order to be able to deal effectively with the demands of the job. Though a master's degree from an ALA-accredited institution is sufficient for most upper administrative positions, some institutions such as colleges or universities require an additional master's or doctorate degree. In most cases, however, it is not an impressive educational background that defines a successful library leader but rather a solid combination of experience and personal attributes.

PROFESSIONAL ASSOCIATIONS

Public Libraries
- American Library Association (ALA)—www.ala.org
  - *Public Library Association (PLA)*
    www.pla.org/ala/mgrps/divs/pla/index.cfm

Academic Health Sciences Libraries
- Medical Library Association (MLA)—www.mlanet.org
- American Medical Informatics Association (AMIA)—https://www.amia.org
- National Network of Libraries of Medicine (NN/LM)—http://nnlm.gov
- Association of Academic Health Sciences Libraries (AAHSL)—www.aahsl.org
- Regional and local health sciences library associations

University Libraries
- American Library Association (ALA)—www.ala.org
  - *Association of College and Research Libraries (ACRL)*
    www.ala.org/ala/mgrps/divs/acrl/index.cfm
- Association of Research Libraries (ARL)—www.arl.org
- Regional and local library associations

Law Libraries
- American Association of Law Libraries (AALL)—www.aallnet.org
- Special Libraries Association (SLA)—www.sla.org
- Regional and local law library associations

STEVE PODGAJNY

Executive Director, Portland Public Library, Portland, Maine

*"The range of concerns and level of accountability
is what makes the director's job unique."*

AT THE top of the Portland Public Library's web page (www.portlandlibrary.com), in bold garnet letters, are the phrases, "Enriching our community. Expanding our world." These slogans are driven by the person responsible for the administration of the main library and the five branches of the public library system of Portland, Maine. This person is Steve Podgajny.

As executive director of the Portland Public Library, Steve has what he calls "global responsibilities." "My job is to find the resources for the staff to be great," he explains, "as well as to place the library board in a position to be successful . . . which, in turn, helps gain resources for the staff. If either the staff or board is ineffective, then I haven't put them in a position to succeed." In addition to his responsibilities for the administration of the main library and its affiliated branches, he is directly responsible for seven senior staff members with whom he communicates as a group as well as individually, depending on the project or plan.

"I am responsible for the general direction of the library system and making sure that direction is in sync with consensus that has come out of planning activities," Steve says. "I articulate that direction to the public and to staff. I pay attention to trends and directions that are evident in the external environment, such as fiscal conditions, information industry developments, or patron behavior changes."

Steve's professional routine varies from day to day. He has many meetings with staff to help plan or facilitate their work. He meets with the public to explain policies or to solicit funds, and is kept very busy facilitating the work of the library board. "It also becomes an ongoing load to deal with e-mail flow that has its own expectations around speed and quality of response," he says. "In addition, I can count on a certain amount of unpredictable events in my daily routine—everything from real emergencies to public relations issues to unexpected opportunities for collaboration."

During the past year, Steve's "normal" routine has been altered considerably by a large-scale renovation project involving the main library. The multimillion-dollar renovation, completed only recently, involved changing the façade of the building, redesigning the front desk areas, and enhancing the comfort, usability, and appeal of the library's public spaces. The goal of the renovation project was to make the library more comfortable and user-friendly, and to focus on user experience. This project was the first phase of an ongoing renovation plan. To keep the public informed of renovation developments, Steve maintains a blog called *Reach for the Stars: Help Us Build the Portland Public Library for the Future* (http://portlandlibraryplans.blogspot .com). The library was closed to the public for six weeks and then hosted a "Reopening Celebration." The schedule of events included a ribbon-cutting ceremony, storytimes for children, author lectures and book signings, and other educational events, all free to the public.

Steve says that he did not structure his career with the intention of becoming an administrator. "I think it was an extension of wanting to make a difference," he explains. "I became a librarian initially because I wanted to work in an environment that dealt with ideas and offered direct service to a variety of users. My interest in administration grew out of both positive and negative experiences as a frontline reference librarian."

Steve received his B.A. in liberal arts from Lock Haven University in Pennsylvania. During that program, he had an assignment that involved conversing with a faculty member about a book on the reading list. He ended up having a conversation with the Lock Haven library director, Bob Brevard, about Thurber's *Carnival*. "The library director really inspired me, though it may have been unintentional," he says. "I am not sure what I thought of librarians to that point, but Bob was a very warm, funny, and engaging guy. He was smart and I remember thinking that he was pretty sharp. That experience kind of hung around in the back of my mind and had a big role in keeping the possibility of working in a library on my inner radar."

After working in business and government for a time, Steve decided to pursue librarianship and enrolled in the M.L.S. program at Clarion University in Pennsylvania. "One thing I did know instinctively in library school was that I enjoyed reference work and wanted somehow to combine it with another love: art history," he says. "My graduate internship in the Art Department at the Carnegie Library of Pittsburgh solidified my interest in the arts and humanities." After working as a reference librarian in several public and community college settings, he "moved on to directorships." Before securing his current position in 2006, he served as director of the Dyer Library in Saco, Maine, for 6 years and as director of the Curtis Memorial Library in Brunswick for 18 years. In 2000 he was named Maine Librarian of the Year in recognition of his distinguished record of professional service to libraries and civic/cultural domains.

Steve relies heavily on technology in his work. "Technology plays a huge role for me," he says. "From e-mail to intranet documents being posted and reviewed or interviewing a candidate on Skype because we can't afford to fly them to Maine, technology is as 'structural' as the heat in the building. When one takes a deep breath and looks back over the record of individual or group work, it is very clear that the productivity is astonishing and is driven by technology." He participates in blogs, Facebook, LinkedIn, and other social networking venues. "The challenge is trying to contain the twenty-four-hour 'bleed' of work into personal time," he says. "Sometimes you have to not be available in order to recharge."

Steve studies as much as he can about consumer technology, lifestyles, and local demographics. "I think exhibits at conferences are a great place not only to see new things but also to connect with colleagues who may have already tried a product or strategy," he says. "The networking piece is critical for library administrators. The support you get during tough times along with good creative thinking on ways forward is priceless. Many times, this networking is what keeps me going." He is a member of the American Library Association, the Public Library Association, the OCLC Global Council, and statewide organizations.

"Public librarianship is different today," Steve maintains, "because many user expectations have changed and are driven by a dynamic consumer environment and social networking. Though ideas are still our staple, the formats and delivery have radically changed or have been amplified."

To those interested in library administration, Steve stresses the importance of learning on the job. "My best managerial and administrative training has come from being a part of other nonprofits and nonlibrary boards and paying attention to colleagues who have been terrific in running organizations," he says. "I have also found that the board leadership that I have been exposed to over the years has been critical in my development. I was well prepared coming out of library school for public services activity. I also had a basic exposure to administration. Other than providing professional context, helping you to be comfortable in your first position, and being confident that you have the soul of a librarian, the rest of your career should be a daily exercise in learning on the job, with library school education becoming increasingly irrelevant."

"Not everyone has the skills or the attitude to be good at library administration," Steve continues. "There is nothing more dispiriting to a staff or publicly damaging than an ineffective administrator." According to him, good administrators should possess the following qualities: optimism, creativity, humor, humility, energy, and respect. They must be good listeners, they must be inspiring and fearless, and they must have a deep and authentic belief in libraries.

"Administrators must be able to handle multiple projects and issues simultaneously," Steve says. "Planning skills are very important, as well as understanding when to back off and when to take a chance. Sometimes you've got to take a chance simply because your gut tells you it is the right thing to do." He says that directors need the ability to balance public expectation and need with an understanding of external factors. "This is difficult but endlessly changing and exciting.

"Understand the basics and uniqueness of libraries," Steve advises, "and sit down for a heart-to-heart with as many administrators as you can. The depth, intelligence, and enthusiasm shown will deeply affect your real-life understanding of administration."

CATHERINE A. QUINLAN

Dean of the USC Libraries, University of Southern California, Los Angeles

*"Successful library leadership requires a personal
investment in the success of your institution."*

IN HER position as dean of the USC Libraries, Catherine Quinlan is responsible for the administration and overall direction of the university's twenty-two libraries, including the main library, the health sciences libraries, and the law library. "My prime responsibility is to provide the best library possible for the University of Southern California," she says. The libraries serve primarily the students, faculty, and staff of USC, which is a private institution. Secondary clientele include academic partners in the state, region, country, and at the international level.

"We also support researchers from around the world that come to USC," Catherine says. "USC's admission standards are very high, so we have a bright, engaging, and inquisitive group of students. Our faculty are active researchers and take seriously USC's interest in achieving excellence on the global stage. These groups constantly challenge us to provide the best collections and services we can with the resources available to us."

When asked about her daily professional routine, Catherine responds, "This is a job that resists routine." She divides her time among broad responsibilities such as raising money, organizing the allocation of resources, establishing partnerships on and off campus, and being a persistent advocate for the value of libraries to the strategic goals of the university. "I establish the things I need to complete each week, and endeavor to complete them amid all the issues that arise," she says. Her efforts are supported by an eight-member Dean's Cabinet, which is comprised of associate deans and executive directors of communications and advancement.

"The most exciting feature of my job," Catherine says, "is the great opportunity I have to make the library relevant to everybody on campus and off. As technology changes, as media evolve, the necessity of creating meaning remains—the necessity of helping our users make sense of the vast world of knowledge that becomes more accessible, but not necessarily more comprehensible, every day. I sincerely believe that the library is the underpinning of everything that happens on this campus, and it has been invigorating to see the enthusiasm with which others have welcomed the library's participation in and support of their academic and research activities. As a library leader, I have a unique opportunity to strive for the libraries to be intriguing, innovative, and integral to all the academic and research achievements of the USC community."

Catherine recognizes that technology is an "important enabler" in her work but says that it should serve as a means to an end. "I believe that technology should serve the purpose of the goal at hand rather than becoming the goal itself," she explains. She is not a frequent user of social networks, but respects their value in reaching library users and in providing service. "Our faculty and staff use wikis internally as communication tools for committee work and the like," she says. "We use blogs, microblogs, and RSS feeds to make information mobile and communicate with our users in places where they seek it. The issue boils down to meaning and relevance. If social web applications help us connect with our community in a way that is meaningful to them, we pursue those opportunities. On the other hand, when situations demand an in-person approach, we provide as much personal interaction as we possibly can."

As is the case for many in the profession, Catherine did not imagine a career as a librarian. She trained as a musician at Queen's University in Kingston, Ontario, and played professionally for a while after earning her bachelor of music degree, but then decided that she did not want to make music her life's work. She applied to law school and library school at the same time at Dalhousie University in Halifax, Nova Scotia, and attended both programs for a short time. "I decided that law school was not a good fit for me, and I enrolled full-time in the library studies program," she says.

"Looking back, I see my path to librarianship as one influenced by diverse interests and aspirations that have served me very well.

"I have been very fortunate in my career," Catherine says. After her first year in library school, she was accepted as a summer intern at the health sciences library at Dalhousie. When the library advertised a full-time professional dental librarian position at around the time she graduated with her M.L.S., she applied and was awarded the position. "I was thrilled," she says. "I worked with some wonderful people who emphasized the service aspects of librarianship, and that focus has influenced many of my career choices in the years since."

During this time, Catherine became interested in operations research and was accepted in the M.B.A. program at Dalhousie. After getting married, she decided to move with her husband to Memorial University in Newfoundland, where she was hired as a part-time cataloger. She transferred to the M.B.A. program there and continued her studies.

"A year or so after my arrival at Memorial, I became the head of the health sciences library when the current head resigned and suggested that I apply for the position," she says. "This was a tremendous increase in responsibility, which I was determined to fulfill. I worked very closely with the dean of medicine, to whom I reported, to ensure the continued development of the library. He also acted somewhat as a mentor to me, suggesting ways in which I could continue to develop professionally. He also included me on many of the planning committees for the faculty, which I greatly enjoyed."

Four years later, Catherine began to think of expanding her horizons. She was eventually hired as the director of libraries at the University of Western Ontario in London, Ontario. "I went from managing a staff of about 20 to running a system employing approximately 250," she says. "I became the youngest university librarian ever appointed in Canada at that time.

"The provost at Western was very supportive and helpful," Catherine continues, "and I think that helped me succeed in the very challenging early 1990s budget situation in the province. A cut of some 45 percent over three years was levied against the libraries and other units. It was with the help of the library faculty and staff and the university administration that we were able to survive—and in some cases, thrive—as well as we did."

After six years at Western, she was recruited by the University of British Columbia (UBC) to serve as the university librarian there. In that position, Catherine headed a library system encompassing 300 full-time staff members and more than twenty-one sites. At UBC she was successful in raising $70 million for the construction of a new building, the Irving K. Barber Learning Centre.

A decade after taking the job at UBC, a search firm contacted Catherine regarding the position she now holds—the dean of libraries position at the University of Southern California. "The USC Libraries recently had been reconstituted as a stand-alone entity, and USC was interested in seeing the libraries grow as successfully as the other academic and research activities on the campus," she says. "The provost and the president got me excited about the position. It has been a great pleasure to be at USC and to help guide the development of the libraries.

"While my professional positions have seen a steady evolution in scope and responsibilities over the years," Catherine says, "the common factor has been the people. For every job, at least one person among the institution's administration or the library's faculty or staff has gotten me intrigued by the position and convinced me of their interest in seeing the libraries excel."

Becoming an upper-level administrator was never Catherine's explicit ambition. Early in her first job as a professional librarian, she grew increasingly interested in how work was done in an efficient and elegant way and in how decisions were made; hence the decision to pursue the M.B.A. Throughout her career, several people in senior administrative positions served as mentors for her. "I have been very fortunate in my career that senior administrators have taken an interest in me and have been willing to give me a chance," she says.

"I got into administration because I was drawn to the work, the potential for achievement on a larger scale, and the possibility of making a tangible difference at my libraries," she continues. "When I interview people for administrative jobs, I am surprised and somewhat disappointed that many are seeking the prestige of a senior position rather than an opportunity to improve the operation of the library or unit. Successful library leadership requires a personal investment in the success of your institution. If you focus too narrowly on the next step up the administrative ladder, you lose the broader perspective that ultimately will enable your success."

Catherine says that not all librarians should strive to become managers. "I once tried to encourage an excellent reference librarian to apply for the position of head of reference," she recounts. "He looked at me and said, 'Why? I am very good at what I do, and I am very happy at doing it.' He was very smart to know both of those things about himself."

According to Catherine, there are three skills that stand out as "utterly essential" for success as a library administrator. "The first is the ability to work the problem and not the person. The second is the ability to say 'no' to someone while leaving open the possibility for that person to return with a potentially better idea. The third is knowing when to stop seeking new information and get down to the business of making a decision. Add those characteristics to standards like flexibility, common sense, optimism, and cheerfulness, and you have a reasonable profile of a skilled administrator."

Catherine keeps up with changing technology and networks with colleagues by attending professional conferences, maintaining contact with friends in the profession, reading articles and journals, and having frequent lunches with USC's chief information officer. She is a member of many professional organizations.

"I believe that the essential meaning of librarianship is the same as it was thirty years ago," Catherine concludes. "What has changed are the methods by which we provide services and access to collections. The volume of information accessible to students and other information consumers has made research and learning tasks more complex. Through promoting media literacy, helping people determine what is an authoritative information source and what is not, and acting as guides to the vast information landscape, I believe that libraries and librarians have become more critical than ever."

GERALD (JERRY) PERRY

Director, Health Sciences Library, Anschutz Medical Campus,
University of Colorado, Denver, Colorado

"I stand on the shoulders of giants, and I am deeply in their debt."

JERRY PERRY says that an essential theme throughout his career has been the significant role that mentors have played. His mentors are the "giants" upon whose shoulders he stands and to whom he is deeply in debt. "I am now trying to pay off that debt," he says, "by giving back to the community of librarianship and by encouraging and supporting the team I am privileged to lead."

That team would be the faculty and staff of the Health Sciences Library (HSL) of the Anschutz Medical Campus at the University of Colorado at Denver. As director, Jerry is responsible for the planning, implementation, and evaluation of all library and information management programs and services offered by the library. This includes the acquisition and licensing of information resources for the campus as a whole. He is also responsible for appointing and directing faculty and staff and for the allocation of library resources in support of campus and library missions and goals.

"I lead by advancing the mission of the library in service to our campus," Jerry says. "As director my focus is essentially external, representing the library to the campus, university, and community leadership." He works closely with the library's deputy director, whose role is to manage the day-to-day operations. "Given the need for coordination, it is crucial that the deputy and director have an excellent working relationship," he says. "I am happy to say that, indeed, HSL's deputy director is an exceptional colleague and coleader. As the HSL is a planning organization, it is essential that all members of our HSL team are coordinated in collectively advancing our mission as detailed in our strategic plan. Five department heads advance the work of the library. Distributed among the departments are just over a dozen faculty members and about two dozen staff."

Jerry typically works a twelve-hour day. He arrives at work at around 8 a.m., logs into the campus network, checks e-mail, and reviews his calendar for the day. "I intentionally schedule time during the day for ongoing initiatives," he says, "and I parse the work I need to do on various projects across time so that I can avoid finding myself simply in reaction mode. Much of the work I do is in drafting reports and proposals, communicating and gathering information, building and maintaining relationships, and representing the possibilities and potentials of the library wherever and however I can." At midday he normally takes lunch at his desk, then spends the afternoon and early evening in meetings, checking e-mail, drafting reports and messages, and preparing for the next day or for later in the week.

"Once home, I make a quick meal (I cook on Sundays for the week) and log on to the Internet to check work e-mail, my private e-mail, and Facebook," Jerry says. "During their respective seasons, I check the Major League Baseball and the National Hockey League websites in order to check on my teams (Rockies, Cubs, Mets, and D-Backs; and Avalanche, Blackhawks, Sabres, and Canadiens)!"

Jerry says that what challenges him the most about his work is also what excites him the most: working and communicating with people. "I am endlessly fascinated by people in all our diversities and how we communicate," he explains. "It is not always easy to communicate effectively or efficiently, and it is not always easy to work with some folks, for whatever reason. But fundamentally I like people and I enjoy working with the tools of communication—especially writing."

Many of the "tools of communication" utilized by Jerry are driven by technology. "I believe that as information workers, contemporary technologies have always played significant roles in what it is that we do," he says. He recalls the manual reference work he did while working as a library assistant in one of his first library jobs, where he searched the literature manually, drafted long lists of references, photocopied articles, and placed them in the mail. He phoned in interlibrary loan requests, typed catalog cards, and dutifully filed them in drawers. "In essence," he says, "I answered my customers' questions; I reviewed, located, and profiled evidence in support of decision-making and scholarship; and I organized and distributed information. The library staff members that I manage today do the same, only they use more expeditious and powerful technologies."

He says that the technologies we use in librarianship are fundamentally about saving time and enhancing convenience; they allow us to expand our capacity for productivity but also allow us to do new things that enhance the utility of information. "But for all the brilliance of smartphones, web applications, social media, and other tools," he says, "it's important to remember that we are information workers and have always used the best technologies available to us in our mission of service. In the end we are about connecting people to the right information when and where it is needed."

Jerry maintains that "working with information by definition requires an affinity with the technologies used to acquire, manage, and disseminate that information. As such, it is critical to keep up with contemporaneous information technologies." He stays current by following new trends in the media and by paying attention to what his peers are doing with technology. "I try to be especially attentive to what early adopters are doing and using," he says. "That includes technologies used by other academics and librarians but also, more generally, teens and young adults. I try to be voracious in gleaning what I think will be useful and important tech-wise, and I very much rely on my network of personal and professional contacts to learn and validate those choices."

To Jerry and to many in the field of library administration, networking with colleagues is essential. He has been an active member of the Medical Library Association (MLA) for many years. "I cannot imagine being a health sciences librarian outside of MLA," he says. "I have a 'home' in the MLA that sustains me and informs my professional practice. Networking is critical, not only to success, but to simply functioning with any degree of effectiveness. Networking in the context of a professional association or society may not be essential for everyone, and I recognize that other social networks—virtual and otherwise—may sustain and provide fulfillment. The role that associations and societies play, in my opinion, is to coordinate and facilitate commonality and sustain the human experience of collegiality."

Jerry's academic background is in the "study of people and communications." He graduated with a dual degree in journalism and anthropology from Syracuse University, and worked for a while as a freelance journalist. "I was interested in writing for magazines, and I was interested in the cultural expressions of religion and the arts," he says. He did odd jobs to make money in Buffalo, New York, but it was "rough going."

While completing his undergraduate degrees, he worked as a student assistant at the general academic library at Syracuse University, accruing about four years of experience. As freelance journalism opportunities grew further and further apart, he decided to leverage his work-study experience and applied for a library assistant position at the Buffalo General Hospital. He got the job and worked there for over five years. "I worked with a terrific director, Ms. Wentsing Liu," he says. "Most of the time we worked as a two-person team; she managed the library and conducted the online literature searches, and I staffed the service desk, did interlibrary loans, circulated items from the collection, and performed other tasks."

As is often the case with librarians, what started as a job to tide Jerry over turned into a career. He was drawn to the excitement and responsibility of helping the library's clinical customers connect to information that mattered in the course of caring for patients. With Wentsing's encouragement and support, he was able to receive financial help from the hospital to enroll in the library science program at the State University of New York at Buffalo. In his first professional position after graduating, he worked in the Reference Department at the Health Sciences Library at the University of Illinois, Chicago (UIC).

"I was at UIC for almost two years, working with an outstanding team of reference and government documents librarians," he says. "I was hired on the same day as my dear friend Susan Thompson, who taught me so much about searching! Developing that skill base proved to be critical for me. At UIC I had a great mentor in Bob Malinowsky, who was a science bibliographer. My position at UIC was tenure-track, and Bob really helped me to better understand the commitments of tenure, the nuances of faculty status, and essentially how to be an academic librarian."

Together, Jerry and Bob published three editions of the reference book called the *AIDS Information Sourcebook* (Oryx Press). "That was in the very late '80s and into the early '90s, a time of crisis for gay community," he says. "That was also when I 'came out' as a gay man, and so my personal identity was greatly impacted by the AIDS pandemic." He became very involved in gay rights activism and wrote numerous articles and essays about health information for and about the lesbian, gay, bisexual, and transgender (LGBT) community.

Jerry next took a job at the library at Rush University in Chicago, where he worked first as an education librarian and later as head of reference. "I made a lot of important and lasting friendships while at Rush," he says. "It was truly a supportive environment, and I was encouraged by the leadership there to expand my perspectives and to blossom professionally." It was while he was at Rush that Jerry began to connect with other LGBT people working in the field. He and his coworkers were inspired to write and informally publish an alternative gay-centric guide to Chicago for a Medical Library Association meeting in the city. Copies of the guide "went like hotcakes" during the meeting. "Through that endeavor, I was able to connect with many other LGBT folks in the association," he says. "That led me to the effort to help convene MLA's LGBT Special Interest Group (SIG). Those were truly heady days of excitement and fear; that act of organizing essentially 'outted' those of us involved to our professional peers, including the leadership who would likely have a hand in hiring any of us in the future."

After ten years at Rush, Jerry decided that he was ready for a change and that he wanted to advance into a more administrative role. He took a job as head of information services at the Arizona Health Sciences Library (AHSL) in Tucson, where he diligently worked to enhance his academic credentials, presenting papers and posters, publishing, and being active at the chapter and national levels of MLA. "I found a lot of joy and energy in working on MLA-related activities, mostly centered around the work of the LGBT SIG but also the Relevant Issues Section of MLA," he says. "That involvement, my active scholarly life, and the support I received from the library's leadership raised my profile nationally." He was soon elected to the MLA Board of Directors, and he was selected to be part of the inaugural cohort of the National Library of Medicine and Association of Academic Health Sciences Libraries (NLM/AAHSL) Leadership Fellows Program.

"By dint of service on the board and my involvement in the Leadership Program, I met a number of outstanding leaders, many of whom evolved into mentors," Jerry says. "Perhaps most important among them was Nancy Roderer, director of the Welch Medical Library at Johns Hopkins University, with whom I was paired as part of the NLM/AAHSL program. Through my relationship with Nancy I was inspired to advance to a directorship position. I was working as a department head and I knew I lacked the broader perspective derived from oversight over multiple library departments. In order to advance, I would need some experience at the assistant or deputy director level."

With the support of Nancy and the leadership of the AAHSL, Jerry was recruited by Director Rick Forsman to serve as deputy director at the Denison Memorial Library, University of Colorado Health Sciences Center in Denver (now called the University of Colorado Denver). "Rick proved to be a brilliant leader and mentor!" he says. "Alas, we only had three years working together, since Rick soon retired. I was promoted to interim director, a position I held through the search and recruitment process to identify a new leader. In 2007 I was named director."

Jerry says that while his library science education gave him a broad understanding and appreciation for many aspects of librarianship, it was his on-the-job experiences that allowed him to garner the tangible skills needed to be a librarian. "I approached my education as an intellectual engagement and experience rather than as a means of specific skills acquisition," he explains. "I went to school at night, and during the day I applied what I was learning. My job was like the lab or clinical component of my education.

"The real learning of how to manage and administrate took place at work, where I observed, listened, and reflected on how I, as a worker, was managed," he continues. "The key lessons I learned were to pay attention; to listen and discern that which is important; to demonstrate personal and professional integrity; to have enthusiasm for the work you are doing; to be encouraging to the people you work with and to yourself; and to learn to enjoy as best as possible the problems that come your way, as counterintuitive as that may seem—a problem enjoyed is one that does not control you. These lessons have served me well as an administrator."

Jerry has additional words of wisdom for those interested in a career in library administration. "Leading a library demands commitment and full-on engagement," he says. "You must care deeply about your customers and about the team you are privileged to lead. You must care about people and have a genuine concern for their interests, aspirations, and perspectives. You must have a passion for information and its transformative effects. It helps to have a sense of humor and, I think, playfulness. Taking joy in what you do goes a long way to assuaging the aches and pains of long workdays and the challenges to finding and keeping a healthy balance in life.

"Leadership roles exist throughout librarianship and are not limited necessarily to management or administration," Jerry concludes. "My advice to the librarian looking to advance into a leadership role is to figure out what it is about information work that you love, and then do that work with as much commitment and enthusiasm as you can muster."

STEVEN J. BELL

Associate University Librarian for Research and Instructional Services,
Temple University, Philadelphia, Pennsylvania

*"It is through planning, strategizing, budgeting, and helping
to build a great team of library workers that I contribute to
what our library offers to the academic community."*

STEVEN BELL is an academic librarian whose responsibilities are primarily administrative. As the associate university librarian for research and instructional services at Temple University, he oversees all public service units, the science library, the suburban campus library, and the Media Services Department. He typically has daily meetings with colleagues from the library and academic administrators from other departments. "Much of what I do is to build relationships with other parts of the organization so we can better accomplish our goals," he says. "I analyze statistics to assess our performance as an organization. I plan a variety of professional development programs. I resolve problems. And when I have some time to think, I try to develop new ideas for services and programs. Most of all, I try to bring good leadership to the areas of the library for which I am responsible."

Steven received his B.A. in liberal arts from Temple University in Philadelphia, where he was an American studies major. Having enjoyed the extensive research and writing involved with his major, he imagined that a career allowing him to practice these skills would suit his talents well. He enrolled in Drexel University's library school program and earned his master's in library science. After graduating, he held several special librarian positions until he decided that he wanted to work in academic libraries. He secured a position as a reference librarian at University of Pennsylvania's business school and eventually took positions as head of access services and then assistant director.

While working at the University of Pennsylvania, Steven earned a doctorate of education with a specialization in higher education administration. He wanted not only to learn more about higher education, but also to obtain skills and credentials that would be useful as an academic library administrator. Learning more about higher education budgeting, law, and other matters proved rewarding and helpful to his career. He later served as director of the Gutman Library at Philadelphia University for nearly ten years, until accepting his current position at Temple University. "I would sum up the evolution of my career over the past thirty years as a progression of positions of increasing responsibility leading to positions in academic library administration," he says. "But no matter what position I've held, I've always made time to answer reference questions and to teach library instruction sessions. Those are the things that I really enjoy about academic librarianship."

What Steven finds most challenging—and exciting—about his job is the fact that he never quite knows what the day will bring. He deals with a wide range of issues for which there may be no precedent, and must handle sensitive situations that require a significant amount of experience to resolve properly. This may involve student complaints, special requests from faculty, arranging tours for visiting librarians, creating a rationale for a new position, completing employee evaluations, preparing for a library survey, or just responding to the crisis of the day. "I really enjoy the pace and the challenges of solving problems and developing good solutions," he says. Steven also enjoys mentoring colleagues and helping them gain experience with research, writing, and giving presentations. He strives to help less experienced librarians to gain more confidence in their abilities, and is always on the lookout for publishing and presenting opportunities for his colleagues.

One of Steven's greatest passions is keeping up with technology. He says, "Technology is a critical part of my job because we depend heavily on it, and I routinely get involved in decision-making about technology." Early in his career, he made it his job to help his constituents keep up with their specialties, and he developed many techniques for doing this more efficiently. However, when he became an academic librarian, he realized that it was no longer sufficient to just keep up with librarianship. "To really keep up effectively as a librarian," he says, "you must go beyond the boundaries of the profession to explore many different peripheral areas—business and management, psychology, learning and pedagogy, information technology, and others. You must also keep up with the field of futurism and trend watching." He says that librarians must be constantly scanning the environment to see what may be coming next.

In 2000 Steven created "Keeping Up," a website designed to help librarians stay abreast of current issues and changing technology in order to remain relevant as information professionals. It persists as a useful and popular website to this day. His first blog, *The Kept-Up Academic Librarian*, filters news about higher education, librarianship, and related fields. In 2004 he cocreated the "Blended Librarians Online Learning Community." This is an online community of thousands of librarians, faculty, instructional designers and technologists, and other academic support personnel "working collaboratively to integrate the library into the teaching and learning process." His latest blog, called *Designing Better Libraries*, grows out of his interest in design thinking and user experience.

Steven's methodologies for keeping up with ever-changing technology include RSS feeds, table of contents alerts, e-mail newsletters, search alerts in aggregator databases and blog search engines, and web page change detection services. He also recommends following the technology sections and columns in the *New York Times* and the *Wall Street Journal,* subscribing to the *MIT Technology Reports,* and being a regular reader of "Mashable" (http://mashable.com) and "TechCrunch" (www .techcrunch.com). "If you are an academic librarian or want to be one," he says, "you should subscribe to my *Kept-Up Academic Librarian* blog because it is an easy way for you to stay up-to-date with news and developments in higher education without getting overwhelmed." He also makes an effort to attend the annual conferences of professional organizations such as the American Library Association and the Association of College and Research Libraries.

"When you graduate from the M.L.I.S. program, what you have learned will quickly become obsolete," Steven says. "It may be 6 days, 6 weeks, 6 months, or 6 years, but over time much of what you learned will be less relevant because our field advances so rapidly. The only way you can avoid becoming obsolete deadwood yourself is to establish a personal and strategic regimen of keeping up, and to keep modifying that regimen as needed over the course of your career. If you manage to do that you will be the most up-to-date professional in any organization in which you work. Keeping up is the greatest investment of your time."

Steven maintains that it is every librarian's responsibility to not only stay up-to-date on new technologies, but also to determine which ones may best serve the library's patrons. He says that Web 2.0 has had a significant impact on librarianship by opening up a variety of possibilities for communication and outreach. As examples, he mentions blogs, video sites such as YouTube, mobile communications such as handheld smartphones, and tools for students such as Blackboard (courseware), smartboards, and clickers. "I try to look at technology as a vehicle for helping us do what we excel at as librarians: connecting people with information and providing the human touch that makes it work well."

For those interested in preparing for a career as an academic library administrator, Steven gives the following advice: "First seek out an entry-level position in an academic library and see if it's a profession that allows you to really enjoy yourself and gives you the opportunity to grow your passion. If you don't find yourself excited about your work and don't look forward to getting to work most days, it's probably not the job for you." He says that once you have determined that you like the academic environment, you must then decide if you would enjoy being an administrator. Do you enjoy supervising others, hiring staff, handling disciplinary actions, and doing evaluations? Can you see yourself working with dissatisfied patrons, listening to their concerns and complaints, and looking forward to resolving the problems that will make their library experience a much better one? Would you like to play a more significant role in helping to guide the future of the library? Are you interested in helping your librarian colleagues to accomplish their work and improve the quality of the service delivery? If you have answered "yes," you will need to look for opportunities to move into a mid-level administrative position such as a department head or assistant department head. "Begin to gain experience with decision-making, budgeting, and supervision," Steven advises. "You might want to find a mentor to help guide your career. Then it's a matter of working on improving your skills, learning new techniques, visiting other libraries to gain insight into best practices, becoming professionally active, attending leadership workshops, and writing and presenting when possible." Finally, he says that if you decide at some point that you'd like to be the director of a college or university library, you might consider earning a master's degree in higher education to help you better understand the inner workings of higher education organizations as well as principles such as tenure, academic freedom, and shared governance. You might even go further and pursue the doctorate in higher education.

To readers of this book, Steven offers this message: "I'm excited that you have chosen to explore a career in librarianship. This is an exciting time to be a librarian. Then again, I've been saying that for the last five years, and I'll probably be saying it for the next twenty or so. But I must be on to something because this profession seems to be more popular than ever. I've been teaching in library science programs for close to twenty years, and I don't recall any time when the classes have been as full as they are now, and with a more diverse group of students than any time in the past. While I'm pleased that you are reading this book, I would encourage you, as you think about librarianship as a profession and career, to go out and visit libraries and talk to the librarians that work there. I don't know of any librarian who would be unwilling to share their experiences, to provide insights into their day-to-day jobs, and to share their thoughts on where they see the profession heading. You can learn a tremendous amount about librarianship by visiting libraries and talking to librarians. But if you do this, allow me to provide one caution. Just like every other profession, this one has its share of individuals who chose the wrong profession but never decided to go elsewhere. So don't be surprised if you run into some librarians and library workers who are bitter or cynical about their work (or you may come across their blogs). Bear in mind it happens in every profession. I want to assure you that the vast majority of librarians love their work and are passionate about what they do. Keep searching until you find someone who may even be able to mentor your career. There are many among us who would be glad to help. At its core, that is what librarianship is all about—helping other people."

If you'd like to learn more about Steven and his current professional activities, he suggests the following websites and blogs:

- http://stevenbell.info (his home page with links to various sites and information)
- www.stevenbell.info/keepup/ (his "Keeping Up" website)
- http://keptup.typepad.com (*The Kept-Up Academic Librarian*)
- http://blendedlibrarian.org (the "Blended Librarians Online Learning Community" website)
- http://acrlog.org (official blog of the Association of College and Research Libraries)
- http://dbl.lishost.org/blog/ (*Designing Better Libraries* blog)

NOTES

1. Brooke E. Sheldon, "Another Look at Leadership," in *The Portable MLIS: Insights from the Experts* (Westport, CT: Libraries Unlimited, 2008).
2. Michael D. Mumford et al., "Leadership Skills for a Changing World: Solving Complex Social Problems," *Leadership Quarterly* 11, no. 1 (2000): 11–35.

INDEX

You may also be interested in

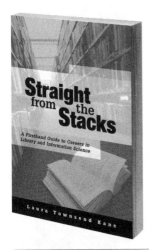

STRAIGHT FROM THE STACKS
A First Hand Guide to Careers in Library and Information Science
Laura Townsend Kane

Tracing career paths, everyday duties, and qualities for succeeding, these spotlights provide perspective from the trenches. Organized by type of institution including public, school, academic, nontraditional, medical/law, and library administration, this useful overview covers the many areas of librarianship and provides practical answers to common questions.

PRINT ISBN: 978-0-8389-0865-5
192 PAGES / 6" X 9"

A LIBRARIAN'S GUIDE TO AN UNCERTAIN JOB MARKET
JEANNETTE WOODWARD
ISBN: 978-0-8389-1105-1

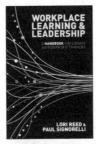

WORKPLACE LEARNING & LEADERSHIP
LORI REED AND PAUL SIGNORELLI
ISBN: 978-0-8389-1082-5

HOW TO STAY AFLOAT IN THE ACADEMIC LIBRARY JOB POOL
EDITED BY TERESA Y. NEELY; FOREWORD BY CAMILA A. ALIRE
ISBN: 978-0-8389-1080-1

WHAT THEY DON'T TEACH YOU IN LIBRARY SCHOOL
ELISABETH DOUCETT
ISBN: 978-0-8389-3592-7

BEING INDISPENSABLE
RUTH TOOR AND HILDA K. WEISBURG
ISBN: 978-0-8389-1065-8

WRITING AND PUBLISHING
EDITED BY CAROL SMALLWOOD
ISBN: 978-0-8389-0996-6

Order today at **alastore.ala.org** or **866-746-7252!**
ALA Store purchases fund advocacy, awareness, and accreditation programs for library professionals worldwide.

ORDER TODAY!

ALA Member # (Must provide to receive your discount.)
☐ home ☐ organization

_____

E-MAIL ADDRESS (REQUIRED in case we have questions about your order.)

Daytime Phone

_____

Ship to

_____
NAME

_____
TITLE

_____
ORGANIZATION

_____
ADDRESS

_____
CITY   STATE   ZIP

METHOD OF PAYMENT
☐ Check or money order enclosed $_____
(Make payable to ALA)

☐ Bill my library, school or organization. (Only orders of $50 or more from established organizational accounts can be billed.)

☐ Purchase Order #_____ (Only for billed orders to libraries, schools or other organizations. First-time customers, please provide organizational purchase order.)

☐ VISA   ☐ MasterCard   ☐ American Express

☐☐☐☐ ☐☐☐☐ ☐☐☐☐ ☐☐☐☐
Credit Card Number

☐☐ / ☐☐
Exp. Date

_____
SIGNATURE

FEDERAL TAX I.D. NUMBER

_____
(Library, Bookstore)

ISBN	Title	qty.	unit price	10% Member discount*	total (qty. × unit price – discount)

METHOD OF SHIPPING
All orders are sent UPS Ground Service unless otherwise specified*. For the following alternate shipping options, call 1-866-SHOP ALA for a shipping quote.

☐ UPS 2nd Day Air (Cost plus $20)

☐ UPS Next Day Air (Cost plus $10)

*AK, HI, Puerto Rico, U.S. Virgin Islands, and Guam orders must select UPS 2nd Day.

Keycode 382010

SHIPPING & HANDLING CHARGES WILL BE ADDED TO ALL ORDERS
Within the U.S.:
Up to $49.99 . . . . $9
$50 to $99.99 . . . . $11
$100 to $149.99 . . . . $13
$150 to $199.99 . . . . $14
$200 to $299.99 . . . . $15
$300 to $999.99 . . . . $20
$1,000+ . . . . . Call 866-776-7252
For bulk rates, call 800-545-2433, ext. 2427

subtotal _____

sales tax ** _____

shipping and handling (see chart above) _____

order total _____

*Member discounts do not apply to special offers or sets. **Discounts are not combined.**
**Residents of IL, CT, DC, GA, or PA who are not tax exempt, please add appropriate sales tax. If you are unsure of your tax rate, call 1-866-746-7252 for assistance. If you are tax exempt, please include a copy of your tax-exempt certificate with your order.
IMPORTANT: Only orders of $50 or more from established organizational accounts can be billed.

For a full selection of ALA Editions products,
visit alastore.ala.org

ALA Store purchases fund advocacy,
awareness and accreditation programs for
library professionals worldwide.

Keycode 382010